I0088683

BEYOND THE SHIFT

Volume One

CHAPTERS AUTHORED BY:

Wendy S. Burton, Karina Del Pezo,
Ingrid Toledo-Hammett, Lucie Miłosz Haskins,
Pamela Hawkins, Sarah Holmes,
Katrina Laflin, Libby Lee, Heather Middler,
Angela Kaye Simon, Tara Winter, Michele Woodburn

Compiled by
PAMELA LEE LYNCH

COPYRIGHT © 2023 by Pamela Lynch

Book Title: Beyond The Shift
Authors: Wendy S. Burton, Karina Garcia Del Pezo, Ingrid Toledo-Hammett, Lucie Miłosz Haskins, Pamela Hawkins, Sarah Holmes, Katrina Laflin, Libby Lee, Heather Middler, Angela Kaye Simon, Tara Winter, Michele Woodburn

ALL RIGHTS RESERVED. SourceCode Publishing and its authors recognize all information, including the material in its sacred texts, comes from the collective consciousness. However, no part of this book may be reproduced by any mechanical, photographic, or electronic process, or in the form of a phonographic recording; nor may it be stored in a retrieval system, transmitted, or otherwise be copied for public or private use without prior written permission by the author.

The intent of the authors is only to offer information of a general nature for your general use and well-being. The material contained in this book is for reference only. Please seek professional or medical advice from your doctor or other professional health care providers. In the event you use any of the information in this book for yourself or others, the authors and the publisher assume no responsibility for your choices or actions.

Disclaimer: This work depicts actual events in the authors' lives. Some places, people, and stories have been altered in these stories to respect and protect the privacy of individuals.

Front Cover Art Design: **Pamela Hawkins**
Proofreader: **Lucie Miłosz Haskins**
Publisher and Editor: **Pamela Lynch, SourceCode Publishing**

ISBN: 978-1-7388950-0-7

DEDICATION

To all the devoted souls who are here to shift the consciousness.

AND to each of the authors who dove into the unknown to write their chapter to help document this shift. Without you this book wouldn't exist:

Wendy S. Burton, Karina G Del Pezo,
Ingrid Toledo-Hammett,
Lucie Miłosz Haskins, Pamela Hawkins,
Sarah Holmes, Katrina Laflin,
Libby Lee, Heather Middler,
Angela Kaye Simon,
Tara Winter, Michele Woodburn

Contents

GRATITUDE

To The Spiritual Entrepreneurs

You have returned on a journey to remember who you are as a soul, and with the goal of doing your part to aid in shifting the consciousness of the planet. You accepted this soul mission knowing the journey would be full of a wide range of experiences, and may even include immense heartache and challenges. This is an expression of gratitude and acknowledgment for your choice to be here on earth during this powerful and important time as we collaboratively co-create this shift. Thank you for saying yes and understanding that the blessings inherent in your desire to expand and change lives are worth it. You are seen, valued, and deeply appreciated.

To The Authors

Within these pages are the stories of twelve authors who courageously said yes to co-authoring this book. As your publisher, I am grateful to each of you for your willingness to share intimate passages of your life. And to reveal the lessons that led to your transformation and expansion into becoming a spiritual leader.

GRATITUDE

To Pamela Hawkins

It is with immense gratitude that we both tapped into the frequency that you were to be the artist to create the cover for Beyond The Shift. As the publisher, I was delighted. The authors, readers, and I appreciate the energy you infused into your painting with intention, light language, codes, and creative flow. You've created a masterpiece.

In Pamela Hawkins' words, "I began with a blank canvas and wrote a prayer for all of the authors, as well as every-one who comes in contact with the book ... the words and stories therein. May you receive what you most need in terms of insights, inspiration, activation."

To You, The Reader and Receiver of this Work

We, the authors and publisher, thank you for receiving this book whether for your intimate exploration of self or to benefit your clients whom you guide on their journey. We hope you find treasures within these words and within yourself as you explore the depths of who you are. May you see and hear yourself and others in the stories, be open to the parts of you ready for your expansion, and know you are not alone on this journey.

INTRODUCTION TO BEYOND THE SHIFT

As an international team of collaborators, we realized early on that inclusion is at the heart of this book and the shift in consciousness.

We intended to embrace the uniqueness within each author's chapter for individual identity, ethnicity, nationality, gender, spelling, language, and style.

This choice is at the core and essence of who we are and is pristine in capturing each author's voice and authenticity. We believe it is necessary for not only the words, but also the energy and wisdom, to also be transmitted and communicated to you, the reader, in its fullness.

"Imagine living in your skin and not fitting into those pronouns." —Katrina Laflin

"Part of decolonizing our world are grammar rules used to reinforce a gender binary that is fake and socially constructed, and doesn't represent a huge portion of the world." —Angela Kaye Simon

WELCOME TO BEYOND THE SHIFT

Dear Reader,

This book is for you, courageous soul, as you willingly remember and express who you came here to become.

Within these pages are **real-life challenges, transformations,** and **teachings to guide you through healing and expansion** along your journey to becoming your most **authentic self**. These stories will begin the inner work for many while contributing to a solution to shift humanity's consciousness.

You may be at the beginning of your awareness, deep into healing, or curious about what others are thinking about our future.

We can no longer tiptoe gently into the unknown. Nor can we linger in the field of fear. Instead, let us be willing to commit to our well-being at a cellular level.

Twelve incredible authors who care deeply about you, and the future of our planet wrote this book for you. Their stories give people a deeper understanding of why, where, and how we will achieve, transform, and transcend into a new way of being.

The foundations for each chapter have been skillfully articulated: Collective Truths. Faith. Spiritual Healing. Mining our depths. Ripping the seams. Our love for the seen, unseen, and unknown. It's taken humanity a long time to recognize we have veered dangerously off path.

WELCOME TO BEYOND THE SHIFT

As we move through this shift in consciousness, each of us is invited to examine our beliefs, limits, and possibilities. We are bravely tearing down the scaffolding that has kept us limited to relay the messages that matter to our future well-being.

The authors' stories are wayshowers for you to navigate loss, indoctrination, disempowering beliefs, and heartache. May you uncover your true essence underneath the protective layers caused by lifetimes of lies, disappointments, and betrayals.

We are not intended to do our healing work in a vacuum and are here to guide each other home. It is my desire as the publisher that you find your guide within these pages, as each author is a spiritual leader in their own right.

It is our intention that you see yourself through the knowingness of the authors, and get a glimpse of your truth and how extraordinary you are. Allow yourself to be wrapped in loving kindness as you read and navigate harsh realities with what may feel both familiar and uncomfortable. Resonating with new understanding and awarenesses, feel the dam within you burst wide open.

As you embark on this journey, know the intention is to reveal to you your potential. And at the deepest level, the grace of who you are—a brave, authentic, and wholeheartedly conscious being.

With love and appreciation for you, the receiver of this sacred wisdom.

Pamela Lynch

A GLIMPSE INTO THE STORIES

Celestial Revelations: A Journey into Interconnected Energies by Tara Winter

Tara invites you on a journey of self-discovery and empowerment as she unveils intrinsic celestial bodies. She illuminates how you can harness these energies to your advantage, which Tara corresponds brilliantly through seven chakras to the outer reaches of our planetary system.

Step Up and Own Your Power: Reject Victimhood and Reclaim Your Personal Power by Katrina Laflin

Katrina's chapter demonstrates how to shift from giving away your power to taking radical responsibility for your role in relationships. Her gift is evident in her authenticity, and guides you to embrace your own Radical Authenticity in what she calls her SoulScape.

The Power of Language and the Meaning You Give It by Sarah Holmes

Sarah helps you notice the words you speak to yourself and others, and make powerful changes to your language from your awareness to an empowered state. Her chapter is intended to nurture and support you in a way that is for your journey and whatever you seek to experience in your life.

Unfuck Yourself: Religious Trauma to Spiritual Freedom by Angela Kaye Simon

A multidimensional and interdisciplinary journey awaits. The destination is an intentionally crafted life of freedom, free of unexamined societal programming. Traversing multi-faceted layers of social conditioning, Angela weaves wisdom and experience as a psychic, sociologist, and spiritual leader to help support the reader to shift and reach the intended destination.

Magickal Crystal Healing by Karina Del Pezo

Learn from a multi-accredited Advanced Crystal Master about how crystal healing works. Karina downloaded a Crystal Door Trifecta which she shares with you in her chapter. You'll learn about the seven main chakras and the crystals that support each along with the properties of specific crystals to create abundance.

Breaking the Chains: A Journey of Healing and Liberation by Ingrid Toledo-Hammett

Ingrid shares insider secrets of a world locked into indoctrination. You will learn what life is truly like growing up in a community that shuns families who break the rules of that system, and the courage it takes to release and rebuild a new life.

The First Cuts Are The Hardest: Gaining Clarity While Living Through Loss by Lucie Miłosz Haskins

After caregiving for her husband for fourteen years, Lucie transformed her loss into loving memories for her and her family. She magically found a way to remember him and wrap themselves up in a treasured gift. Lucie reminds us all that love truly is the most powerful force in the universe.

Reconnect With Your Inner Compass by Libby Lee

"Reconnect With Your Inner Compass" is not only a chapter in this brilliant book but a testament to Libby's dedication to helping souls shine as the radiant stars they were born to be. Dive into its pages and discover the secrets to aligning to your own authenticity and transforming your journey into one of profound impact and fulfillment, one choice at a time.

Magical Moments: Finding the Sweet Spot in the Power of Telepathy by Heather Middler

During her daughter's final days, messages with end-of-life desires were received clearly by Heather. Going forward, she was able to help people navigate the transition of a loved one. Heather's telepathic abilities allow her to pass along messages from the spiritual realm.

Angel Power: Enlist the Help of Your Angels to Create Play, Joy, and Abundance by Wendy S. Burton

After publishing her first book, Amy and the Angels, the most common question Wendy was asked was "How do I connect to my Angels and manifest the things I want?" Her chapter teaches you the three steps to connect with your Angels.

The Crone in The Labyrinth by Michele Woodburn

Michele's journey through faith and the spiritual patriarchy led to a joyful reclaiming of The Crone after millennia of persecution and suppression. She weaves a fascinating story as she navigates life through the journey inwards and outwards along a labyrinth path to the outer reaches, returning home towards the center as The Crone.

Revealing by Pamela Hawkins

It takes tremendous courage to navigate the depths of who we are and who we're becoming in this shift in consciousness, yet this is exactly the invitation Pamela extends in her chapter. As we continue to explore and be curious and nurture our pioneering spirits, more and more will naturally be revealed.

CELESTIAL REVELATIONS
A Journey into Interconnected Energies by Tara Winter

As I embark on this chapter, I am compelled to share with you the journey that led me here. I have been tuned in and tapped in for as long as I can remember. Seeing spirits was my first memory at the age of five.

You see, as a young child, I was a dreamer—quite literally!

I recall nights when I would awaken in the dead of night, sneakily creeping to the living room couch, and there I'd sit, gazing intently through the big picture window at the roadmap of stars.

Deep within me was a belief that I could manipulate those twinkling wonders with the sheer power of my thoughts, and to my astonishment, I did! I fancied myself as an orchestra conductor, but in the '70s, it was more like rocking out to a composition of *We Will Rock You*.

Enveloped in this enchanting stellar energy, I didn't understand the real significance of those magical moments. Nor did I realize what the spirit was showing me at the time.

As I've grown older, it has become abundantly clear that my purpose on this earthly plane is to facilitate the comprehension of these energies. To unveil the intrinsic of celestial bodies and illuminate how we can harness these energies to our advantage.

BEYOND THE SHIFT

Today, I work as an intuitive astrologer, an energy reader, and a healer. I have helped many people become conscious of energy in a way that has changed their lives.

Step into this mind-bending realm where creation unfolds in ways that'll leave your head spinning. Imagine this dance, where energy and time tangle in mesmerizing complexity, offering us a front-row seat to a show of limitless possibilities.

These interconnected energies are like an ever-resonating hum, a vibe that guides us through the twists and turns of this wild ride we call life. It's like a map of possibilities laid out just for your soul to explore.

And check this out—these timelines are not just separate lines on a spreadsheet. No, they're like this crazy intricate web of interdependence. Imagine one thought as a pebble dropped into a pond, sending ripples that touch every corner of the water. That's what happens in this web—one thought, one choice, and BOOM, timelines are shifting like mad.

But hold on, let's talk about the fuel that powers this whole show. It's like the secret sauce of the universe, an elixir that defies logic. This energy is what breathes life into every thought and intention. It's like the heartbeat of consciousness itself.

You might have heard the buzzword "co-creation" being thrown around in the spiritual world.

Sounds cool, right? But what is it really about? It's all about crafting something amazing out of thin air. It's tapping into universal energies and the codes that awaken the magic within us.

When these activation nodes light up, we get the power of choice. We can either dive in headfirst or just watch from the sidelines. That's the real deal with co-creation. Every choice, every move, it's like painting a stroke on the canvas of reality.

Now, picture this.

There are these pivotal moments, these big neon signs on your timeline. They're like game-changers, the Choose Your Own Adventure moments of your life. And guess what? The astrological stars align to give you a nudge in the right direction. One thought, one action at these nodes, and you set off a chain reaction that echoes through time and space.

But let's talk colors, my friends.

The spectrum of these timelines is like an emotional rainbow. From pitch-black obsidian to soothing pastels, each shade reflects a different vibrational energy. Dark hues carry the weight of struggles, while the light ones? They're like a cool breeze on a summer day.

Here's the kicker—can we bend the rules of time? Can we hop timelines with our thoughts? The short answer: yep, mindfulness. Being fully present in the moment helps you tune into the energetic currents. It's like being the captain of your ship in this sea of possibilities.

Amidst it all, remember this—resilience is your superpower.

BEYOND THE SHIFT

You can take a timeline that's wavering and infuse it with rock-solid belief and intent. But these timelines are as delicate as a spider's silk. Negative thoughts? They're like a wrecking ball, smashing your dreams into smithereens.

So, here's to the real deal on the timelines and the crazy universe we're all a part of. Buckle up because this ride's just getting started!

Alright, let's dive deeper into this journey. Imagine we all have these hidden activation points inside us, like secret buttons that connect us to the frequencies of the stars. And these activations? They're like the codes that shape our reality.

Now, where do you find these activation nodes?

Well, I've got a theory. Think of the celestial bodies—planets, stars—as storytellers. Each one's spinning its own tale. But it's not just about storytelling. These beings pack an energetic punch as activation nodes themselves.

You've got some people diving into ancient rituals, stuff passed down through generations. Others are like energy sponges, soaking up vibes from the universe.

Ever notice how people buzz when a full moon's on the horizon? It's like everyone's on high alert. Kids are bouncing off the walls and hospitals are preparing for action. All because of those lunar vibes.

The Solar Plexus of the Sun and Mars

Now, let's zoom in on the Sun and Mars. They're the big shots, and they have a thing for your solar plexus—that's the power center in your upper belly. The Sun, that big ball of radiant energy, has a handshake with your solar plexus. It's as if the sun's saying, "Hey, let's light up your personal power, confidence, and vitality!"

When you tap into this solar connection, it's like you're in harmony with the universe's rhythm. Imagine finding this hidden stash of strength inside you, waiting to bust out. It's like discovering your own superhero powers. As you embrace this solar energy, your inner glow beams brighter, lighting your path and giving you a new sense of direction.

And then there's Mars—the fiery warrior planet. It's like the solar plexus's personal cheerleader but in red-hot flames. Mars channels that fierce energy, igniting your inner strength and determination. Picture a blazing fire, ready to take on anything. That's what your solar plexus feels when Mars's energy shows up.

So, Mars is like that friend who nudges you, saying, "What's your next move, huh?" It's all about action, taking charge, and facing challenges head-on. That fire inside you? It's ready to burn through obstacles like a boss.

But let's not forget the balance.

The solar plexus energy is all about power, purpose, and transformation. When it's singing in tune, you're strutting through life with confidence. But when it's out of whack, shame creeps in like an unwanted guest crashing the party. That shame might come from past baggage, old wounds, or life's curveballs.

You don't have to stay stuck. These activation nodes? They're like guideposts, leading you back to your inner strength. When self-doubt or uncertainty creeps in, the Sun's light and Mars' fire are there to remind you of your untapped power. You're not just a spectator; you're a co-creator of your own story.

Now, you're probably wondering how you can tap into this solar and Martian energy. Well, there's no need for a rocket ship. Start simple. Bask in the sun's rays and let them charge you up. Or grab a candle and let its flame reflect that fiery Mars energy. And when you're talking to yourself, toss in some "I can" affirmations for good measure.

So, embrace that solar plexus energy, let the Sun and Mars fuel your fire, and remember—you're not just watching this show, you're writing your own blockbuster.

Time to shine!

Mercury and Your Throat Chakra

Mercury, the speedster of the planets, is wired for communication and quick thinking. This planet's like the universe's chatterbox. Its activation energies have a hotline to your throat chakra.

Imagine Mercury's like that friend who's always got the perfect comeback, who never misses a beat. Your throat chakra is like the microphone for your thoughts. Now, brace yourself for the connection between them.

When you sync up with Mercury's energy, it's like you've got the gift of gab. Your words flow like a river, and your thoughts string together like a symphony. Suddenly, you're this eloquent wordsmith painting pictures with your words. It's like having a thesaurus in your brain.

But here's the magic—it's not just about the words you say. It's about the connections you make and the bridges you build with your words. When your throat chakra's in harmony with Mercury's mojo, you're not just talking, you're communicating. You're sharing ideas, sparking conversations, and leaving a trail of wisdom in your wake.

So, how can you work with this Mercury–throat chakra duo? Well, it's simple, really. Start by talking. Yep, that's it! Engage in conversations, share your thoughts, and listen to others.

And don't forget the power of writing. Keep a journal. Jot down your thoughts, your dreams, your ideas.

Now, for the bold ones out there. Let's talk about public speaking. Yeah, I know it can be nerve-wracking, but think about it. When you stand up and let your voice be heard, you're in sync with Mercury's energy. It's like you've harnessed the planet's quicksilver vibes for your own performance.

Here's the golden rule. Communication isn't just about talking. It's about listening too. So, when you're in conversations, really tune in. It's like your throat chakra isn't just a transmitter, it's a receiver too.

So, embrace the Mercury–throat chakra connection. Let your words flow, share your ideas, and be the cosmic communicator you were born to be. It's like you've tapped into the universe's Wi-Fi, and the signals are strong. Time to chat and let your throat chakra be in harmony with Mercury's lightning-speed energy!

VENUS' HEART

Venus, the cupid of love and beauty. This planet's like the universe's ultimate matchmaker. It's got a special connection and activation node with your heart chakra.

Venus is like that friend who's always setting up perfect dates, creating romantic vibes everywhere it goes. And your heart chakra is like the love command center within you.

When you sync up with Venus's energy, it's like you've got a love potion in your heart. You radiate love, compassion, and kindness like a lighthouse. Suddenly, you're this walking love story, and people can't help but be drawn to your warm and understanding aura. It's like your heart's become a love magnet.

But here's where the magic gets real. It's not just about romantic love. It's about compassion, understanding, and connection. When your heart chakra harmonizes with Venus's vibes, you're not just feeling the love, you're spreading it, too. It's like a ripple effect. You share love, which bounces back to you, creating this beautiful cycle of positive energy.

So, how can you work this Venus–heart chakra magic in your life? Simple. Start by loving yourself. Yeah, that's the foundation. Treat yourself with kindness, embrace your quirks, and celebrate your awesomeness. It's like your heart chakra's receiving a big hug.

And here's the cool part—share that love vibe with others. Smile at strangers, lend a helping hand, be a good listener. It's like your heart chakra's turned into a love transmitter, sending out beams of positivity.

Now, when it comes to relationships, whether romantic or platonic, let your heart lead. Make choices that resonate with your heart's desires. It's like you're following Venus's guide to love, creating connections that are genuine and beautiful.

The secret ingredient is GRATITUDE. Practice gratitude for the love in your life. Let your heart swell with gratitude for these connections, whether it's a special someone, friends, family, or even a pet. It's like fuel for your heart chakra's love fire.

Let your heart radiate love, compassion, and kindness. Share the love vibe with the world, create connections that warm your soul, and let your heart chakra channel in harmony with Venus's enchanting energy.

Jupiter, the Crown Jewel

Jupiter! This bad boy is like the universe's Santa Claus, gifting us with abundance and all-around good vibes. And guess what? It's got a VIP pass to your crown chakra.

Jupiter is like that generous friend who always brings extra snacks to the party. The crown chakra is like the command center, your portal to higher consciousness. When you tap into Jupiter's energy, it's like hitting the jackpot. You're in sync with abundance, riding the wave of expansion. Suddenly, you're this beacon of optimism, and opportunities seem to pop up like confetti.

But it's not just about getting stuff. It's about growth, wisdom, and connecting with your higher self. When your crown chakra is activated by Jupiter's mojo, you're not just climbing the ladder, you're ascending the staircase of consciousness.

Your crown chakra is like a wisdom well, drawing from the universe's knowledge bank. You're tapping into your inner guru, gaining insights that make you go, "Whoa, I never thought of that!" It's like leveling up in the game of life.

So, how can you activate Jupiter and the crown chakra? Simple, seek knowledge. Dive into books, take up a course, and expand your horizons. It's like your crown chakra's on a quest for wisdom, and the universe is your treasure map.

And hey, here's a fun one—stargazing. Yeah, you read that right. Jupiter's a prominent player in the night sky, and its energy's up for grabs. So, get out there, look up, and connect with the largest planet in our cosmic neighborhood. It's like getting a direct line to Jupiter.

The golden rule is to stay open. Stay open to new experiences, new ideas, and new perspectives. Let your crown chakra be the gateway to your expansion. Seek wisdom, open your mind, and ride the wave of abundance.

Saturn, Your Root

The architect—Saturn! This planet's like the universe's master builder, all about structure and discipline. It has an activation node in your root chakra, the very foundation of who you are.

Saturn is like that wise old tree with roots digging deep into the earth. And your root chakra? It's like the anchor that keeps you steady. When you sync up with Saturn's energy, you've got a solid foundation under your feet. You're in tune with structure, discipline, and the power of manifesting dreams. Suddenly, you're a force to be reckoned with, standing tall even when the storm's raging.

It's not just about standing still. It's about growth, resilience, and creating a sturdy base for your dreams. When your root chakra taps into Saturn's vibes, you're not just weathering the storm, you're planting seeds that will grow into massive trees of achievement. So many people in their quest for higher states of consciousness avoid the root because it is a "lower vibration." This is a big mistake, and it hinders so many from achieving their highest timelines.

Your root chakra is like a GPS, guiding you through the twists and turns of life. You're rooted, but your dreams are shooting for the stars. It's like building your own skyscraper, floor by floor, with Saturn as your project manager.

So, how can you tap into this Saturn–root chakra magic? Simple. Get organized. Set goals, make plans, and follow through.

And here's a pro tip for grounding exercises. Yep, it's like giving your root chakra a spa day. Walk barefoot on the earth, meditate, and connect with nature. It's like your root chakra's getting a direct line to Saturn's stabilizing energy.

The key word with this activation node is Patience. Saturn's all about the long game. So, when challenges come your way, remember, you're like that wise old tree—strong, rooted, and ready to weather whatever comes your way.

Let your root chakra be your anchor, keeping you steady as you reach for the stars. Set goals, stay disciplined, and let Saturn's energy be your guide. You're the architect of your dreams, and with Saturn's support, you can build your empire. Time to stand tall and let your root chakra be in harmony with Saturn's structured energy!

THE EYE OF NEPTUNE

Neptune is like that enigmatic sage who holds the knowledge of the cosmos. Your third eye chakra? Think of it as your celestial telescope, peering into realms beyond comprehension. Brace yourself for the ethereal dance between them.

When you align with Neptune's energy, it feels as though your intuition is magnified tenfold. You find yourself in tune with the elusive rhythms of the universe, deciphering mysteries like an interstellar detective. Suddenly, you transform into an intuitive savant, grasping truths beyond the obvious.

But it's more profound than mere knowledge. It's about channeling divine wisdom, discerning the profound truths camouflaged in everyday occurrences. When your third eye chakra resonates with Neptune's aura, you're not just observing, you're perceiving on a cosmic scale.

Your third eye chakra becomes your compass through the vastness of dimensional realms. You're interpreting symbols, sensing energies, and bonding with realities that lie beyond our normal sight.

So, how can you harness this Neptune–third eye synergy in your life?

The key is meditation. Embrace tranquility, concentrate on your third eye, and let your intuitive currents surge. It's akin to tapping into the universe's eternal frequency.

Heed your dreams. Neptune governs the depths of the subconscious, making your dreams its sanctuary. Maintain a dream diary, interpret the symbols, and discover the messages Neptune whispers to you. It's like engaging in a clandestine dialogue with the cosmos.

Believe in yourself. Neptune encourages a deep dive into your soul's ocean. So, when your intuition beckons, pay heed. When this cosmic alignment between Neptune and your third eye chakra materializes, clarity emerges, illuminating every nuance.

PLUTO AND YOUR SACRAL CHAKRA

This enigmatic dwarf planet operates like the universe's private detective, delving deep into concealed truths and traversing the mysterious. And it shares an intimate alliance with your sacral chakra.

Pluto embodies that confidante who ceaselessly delves beneath the surface, forever curious. As for your sacral chakra, it's the pulsating heart of your emotions and creative spirit. Brace yourself for the enthralling synergy between them.

Tapping into Pluto's aura feels like unlocking the universe's most classified archives. You find yourself revealing hidden layers, navigating the profound seas of emotion, and charting the limitless expanse of your imagination. In this dance, you emerge as an astral voyager wandering through dimensions yet to be mapped.

Yet, the true enchantment lies here, transcending mere revelations of secrets. It beckons the acceptance of your shadow, those facets you may have concealed from the world and yourself. When your sacral chakra dances to Pluto's rhythm, you're not merely sensing emotions, you're embarking on profound inner journeys, unearthing treasures of the soul.

Visualize this: your sacral chakra is akin to a reservoir, brimming with emotions, passions, and the sparks of creation. As you align with Pluto, you unlock its gates, allowing emotions to cascade and supercharging your creativity. This alignment sets forth a veritable vortex of self-expression.

Here's how to harness this Pluto–sacral chakra alchemy:

Dive deep into your feelings. Acknowledge them, channel them, and realize they chart your astral narrative. It's as if your sacral chakra crafts your emotional map while Pluto serves as the seasoned navigator.

Express yourself creatively, whether it's through painting, dancing, penning down thoughts, or any artistic venture—unleash that innate creativity. Imagine your sacral chakra as the canvas of the cosmos, with Pluto acting as the brush, painting layers of intricate depth.

Champion transformation. After all, Pluto stands as the sentinel of metamorphosis and rebirth. View adversities as gateways to evolution. Your sacral chakra embodies this transformative cocoon, giving rise to celestial metamorphoses.

So, immerse yourself in the mesmerizing confluence of Pluto and your sacral chakra. Let this chakra be your portal to emotive and creative depths, guided by Pluto's profound resonance. Feel, innovate, and evolve.

In this chapter, I have started to uncover the infinite energetic codes and possibilities. I challenge you to start to sit with these energies and see how your life changes as you consciously work with these energies and the nodes.

As we shift our consciousness, we understand that we are creator beings. We can create something exquisite that extends far beyond the confines of our imagination. It is an invitation to transcend the boundaries of linear thinking to embrace the multidimensional nature of our consciousness and to wield the creative power that resides within each of us.

By tapping into this creative power, we can unlock infinite possibilities and manifest a reality that is truly extraordinary. It is a journey of self-discovery and empowerment, where we realize that our potential goes far beyond what society has conditioned us to believe. As we step into this new paradigm, we open ourselves up to a world of magic and wonder where anything is possible, and our dreams become our reality.

ABOUT TARA WINTER, AUTHOR

I am an intuitive energy reader, astrologer, and healer who has a natural gift for connecting with the unseen world. I bring through messages from your guides, past loved ones, and pets, providing you with comfort, closure, and validation.

I have studied under world-renowned astrologers and energy readers, honing my skills and gaining a deep understanding of energy and alignment.

If you're looking to embark on a journey of self-discovery and expansion, I am here to guide you.

To learn more about your birth chart and to get a reading you can head to my web page:

https://simplytara.my.canva.site/

STEP UP AND OWN YOUR POWER
REJECT VICTIMHOOD AND RECLAIM YOUR PERSONAL POWER BY KATRINA LAFLIN

"No one can make you feel inferior without your consent."
—Eleanor Roosevelt

She is a wise First Lady and is credited with the quote. I'll take this idea a step further: No one can MAKE you feel ANYTHING without your permission.

It might be hard to hear. I know it was for me. I mean, how ridiculous! When someone says or does something that is hurtful to me, certainly that's their fault, right? They're doing and saying this stuff and they are making me feel the things. Or are they?

When I finally let it sink in that I'm actually responsible for my emotions, it was a bitter pill. I should clarify, not for the actual emotions. I mean, we feel what we feel, right? You can't just decide not to feel certain emotions—the feels happen. What you are responsible for is how you choose to react to those emotions and for the resulting actions you choose in response to what you feel. Read that again.

You and only you are responsible! And in that responsibility rests your Power!

Through taking responsibility for your emotions and choosing your response, you own your Personal Power! YOU OWN IT! Your very own Personal Super Power!

STEP UP AND OWN YOUR POWER

I was first introduced to this concept at an Al-Anon meeting. If you're not familiar, Al-Anon is a recovery program for those impacted by the alcoholism of someone in their life. In my case, it was a boyfriend I had been with for nearly ten years—yep, ten years—I'm a slow learner!

As a functional alcoholic, he could hold down a job and maintain appearances in public if people didn't look too closely. He eventually started abusing prescription drugs and doing a lot of self-medicating. He was an alcoholic and drug addict. Plain and simple. And I was the enabling girlfriend. We were a textbook Dr. Phil episode.

I was the definition of a codependent, enabling, emotionally abused partner. I fell into the trap of believing everything he told me about myself. He peppered in just enough positive, complimentary things to wash over all the nasty, mean messages. I remember wishing at one point he would just hit me because that's where I would definitely draw the line. Yes, for sure, being emotionally abused wasn't enough. I had to have some bruises, and it was just words and stuff, right? I felt like what I was going through wasn't really abuse, or not abusive enough. It's not like he actually hit me, because he knew that was a line he couldn't cross. He was smart like that. How messed up is that? I mean seriously, how did I let myself be that person? It was so dysfunctional. Looking back, it feels like a completely different life. I was an addict too, only my addiction was to drama.

I bought into the romanticized idea that the more you suffer, the more it shows you really care (hat tip to Offspring). And if you do all the right things and with enough love, you can turn it around and live happily ever after, like in the movies. What a load of crap! But I was living in it, playing my part as a victim so perfectly. Hindsight being what it is, I was a complete shit show!

When I finally realized I wanted out for real, I still couldn't bring myself to just walk away. I was under his spell of narcissistic manipulation and being told all the things. *I couldn't do better. Nobody would love me like he did. I didn't DESERVE better, and I'd find no one else.* I bought into it. That's how eroded my self-worth was, even when in my mind I recognized I needed to get out. Emotionally, I didn't know how to make that move.

During that relationship, I realized my self-esteem was in the gutter because I wasn't taking responsibility for anything. I was playing the victim, buried in self-hate, playing the blame game. And I was a master!

When I started to really dig into the origin of all my self-doubt and negative self-talk, it took me back to elementary school. Very early on, I perceived I was both not enough and too much all at the same time. It's not like my parents told me these things, as I had a typical rural upbringing as an only child. I just looked at myself with judgmental eyes and blamed outside influences—parents, bullies, and incompetent teachers. In the end, I realized it was all me, and I took my power back.

Let's be honest, in the '70s bullying was 'just the way it was' and I needed to get over it. Well, I didn't get over it and it took a very long time to move past it with a lot of healing and forgiveness.

STEP UP AND OWN YOUR POWER

A little piece of me still hopes karma comes around sooner rather than later on those mean girls. But I'll leave that to the Universe because nobody lives rent-free in my head!

I was the stereotypical victim. Everything was because of everyone else and everything else. I was letting all the outside influences create my life and pointed my finger in every direction when, in reality, all responsibility rested with me. I was the only one who could change the trajectory of my life. But life wasn't fair (duh!) and I fully embraced the victim mentality of that unfairness. I wasn't being intentional, and lacked gratitude and empathy to see how good I had it.

It felt easier to wallow in victimhood than dive deeply into the soul work toward understanding who I really was and what an authentic life looked like for me. Moving beyond the 'supposed to', and being unapologetically myself, felt terrifying and impossible!

When I took a step back and started to really look at my life, I knew none of it was right. I knew I was better than this, because on paper I was a badass rockstar! Smart. Successful. Owner of a profitable small business. I was raising my son on my own and was active in my community. People genuinely liked me. But there was that piece of me that thought unless a man desired me, I was worthless.

Can you relate to this energy of patriarchy?

This was the overall message from my community while I was growing up. Your value rests with the opinions of others and you need to do everything you can to be accepted and liked, even if that means being untrue to your authentic self.

Then one day, the exhaustion of playing my part finally caught up with me and I admitted to myself that I was so tired of the drama. I was tired of running around trying to make someone else happy. I was exhausted from walking on eggshells and wondering when the next drunken meltdown was coming. All the while sacrificing things that were important to me in hopes of 'proving' my fealty.

If you are a fan of movies and tv shows set in the medieval era, you know that fealty is used when a king or lord demands allegiance, loyalty, and devotion from a peasant. And that's exactly how the situation felt. The 'lord of the manor' demanded my fealty and gave nothing in return.

Once I realized I was done with that victim mindset and that I was leaving the relationship, I took time to get my ducks in a row and build my confidence to make the move. It was a journey of self-discovery that I'm still on.

Are we ever NOT on a journey of self-discovery?

I took classes, read books, attended Al-Anon, and spoke to a therapist. Doing all the things to get my footing to figure out answers to the big questions:

Who Am I?
What Do I Want?
What Is My Purpose?

Have you asked these questions of yourself? If so, I bet you felt weight and magnitude similar to what I felt when I asked myself. They seem so simple on the surface. But as you go deeper into the answers, into yourself, the journey can feel overwhelming, in a good way.

And my shift in attention did not go unnoticed. My ex challenged me when he could tell that something was changing with me—in me. He could sense that I was no longer committed to maintaining an even keel to keep the peace, no matter what it took out of me. He could feel his manipulative grasp on me slipping, and that caused him to really act out to demand my attention. In the past, that would have worked. But inside the sphere of the soul work I was doing, his words were losing their power. His demands carried less meaning. I was no longer concerned with his serenity because I learned that my own was no less important than his.

That's the thing about a journey of self-discovery people don't talk about. When you start making changes, it makes other people really uncomfortable. Most people like the status quo, especially if it's working for them. Especially if they have been directly benefiting from you being in a state of disempowerment.

As I was stepping into my power, I was no longer playing my part in enabling his behavior and making excuses. He told me I was being selfish and only worried about myself. Damn straight! If I wasn't going to worry about myself, nobody else was going to! You can't count on a manipulative narcissist to look out for you. EVER! And all this pushback reinforced my knowing that it was my time and I needed to get out.

The Al-Anon meetings were a huge awakening for me and a catalyst for major shifts in my emotional health. I didn't attend for long, maybe three to four months total and not every week, but during that time, I had some major revelations. That program introduced me to the concept of detachment. What a powerful, life-changing concept that was for me! I can still feel the sensation of physical weight releasing and lifting off my body when I heard the words.

I was sitting in a beanbag chair in the church's children's library where our small breakout group was meeting. And it happened.

Someone said IT.

They said, "It is neither my right nor responsibility to suffer because of the actions or reactions of other people."

Not my RIGHT or RESPONSIBILITY.

Meaning I wasn't responsible for my boyfriend's actions or reactions in any way. And beyond that, it was not my RIGHT to take on that responsibility. It was a disservice by making excuses for him and keeping the peace between him and all the other people in his life. I didn't have to respond to his demands and remain emotionally entangled. I could disengage and let him take responsibility for the consequences of his actions. He was responsible for the situations he was creating. I enabled his addiction by not gifting him the opportunity to take responsibility and learn the lessons meant for him in these situations. It never occurred to me that I could disengage and let the consequences unfold, because they were not my consequences.

They were neither my right nor responsibility.

That was seventeen years ago as I write this. I still don't have the words to fully describe the sense of freedom I felt in that moment when I heard those words and they really settled in. I was only responsible for my own actions and reactions. Nobody else's. Just my own. And that was the day I started living more mindfully and taking a pause before reacting to my own emotions. That was a lot easier said than done.

That was my moment of EMPOWERMENT!

In that moment, I took my personal power back and stopped playing The Victim. I started the long journey of understanding and processing my emotions rather than just reacting to the shitty feelings. I began to recognize when the rage, guilt, and shame were rising.

No matter what the situation was or who was inconvenienced by the pause, I learned to give myself a moment to gather, regroup, and disengage. Sometimes that meant literally walking away from the situation. Leaving it unresolved until I had an opportunity to not just process the emotions I was feeling, but to understand why I was feeling them. Nine times out of ten, it wasn't the actual circumstance in the moment. The emotions were a reaction to something that had happened in the past that formed a warped impression in my mind.

I stopped giving my power away, stopped reacting, and started choosing carefully discerned responses.

It wasn't easy, but I had to take these steps toward discovery to find out who I really was down deep.

The emotions were raw and painful. I remember feeling the overwhelm and confusion of trying to understand what I was feeling and why I was feeling it.

It literally took days in the beginning, and my former boyfriend had no patience with the pauses I was taking. He wanted immediate engagement. When I would try to take the time, he would pursue me and demand interaction. When I took the time I needed to process an incident, usually days, he would accuse me of rehashing old bullshit when I would bring up the previous conversation.

I didn't have the words to explain that it took me days to understand why I was feeling what I was feeling—to really get to the root of why. I also didn't feel emotionally safe in that relationship to talk it through, because I knew he would attack me and throw my words in my face. The time I needed to process was noted as a deficiency and failure as a human being. All because I need to take a beat to understand myself. It took me time to dig down and identify where the emotions were rooted. He refused to give me time, and that was one more reason I needed to get out of that toxic relationship.

Around this time, I also learned that my emotional constipation was a consequence of nature and nurture. I honestly believed, to my bones, that I did not have the right to emotions. I needed to suck it up, get over it, and move on. No need to dwell on feelings. That was for wimps!

I discovered through energy work and chakra alignment with a holographic repatterning expert that these beliefs were handed down genetically from both my maternal and paternal sides, going back two and three generations. Those tools, along with the power of numerology, helped me to understand more about who I am and my potential.

STEP UP AND OWN YOUR POWER

Being raised by people who also carried this DNA resulted in an inability to process my emotions quickly. It prevented me from making a calculated and informed choice of action.

I simply reacted without understanding WHY I was feeling what I was feeling. I felt hurt, so I lashed out without fully understanding WHY I felt hurt. Without fail, that hurt originated in events in my very early, formative years and not the current events. It stemmed back to feelings I never fully processed.

Once I realized this, I could notice when these emotions would rise up. Rather than react, I learned to pause to understand why those emotions surfaced and intentionally choose an action in response.

What it comes down to is you are responsible for your feelings and emotions. Nobody can 'make' you feel anything.

I'm not saying you can CONTROL your emotions, like never feeling sad or angry or disappointed or hurt. You want to feel those emotions because in them are the lessons to learn about yourself. And those are the emotions that contrast with happiness, joy, and accomplishment to make these feelings deeper and more enjoyable. I'm saying you get to choose how you respond to those less comfortable emotions.

But first you must process them and understand them.

You need to drill down to the root cause of why you feel hurt or angry or whatever. By placing blame for your emotions on the words or actions of others, you are giving away your personal power. To truly stand in your personal power, you need to take responsibility for your emotions, process them, and make an informed response.

You have no control over other people, their words, actions, choices, or decisions. You only have control over your actions in response to those things. In my mind, I make a differentiation between a reaction and a chosen response. This feels significant to me. To 'react' implies little contemplation and an impulsive retort. But a chosen action is thoughtful and intentional in direct response to the situation at hand.

So, manage your expectations of other people and manage your reactions to their energy.

Playing the victim by blaming how you feel about circumstances and other people is letting them control you. You can control your response and that's all you can control.

You can choose to disengage. You can choose to take whatever time you need to filter through your emotions and understand where they are coming from. And then you can choose an appropriate response, or no response at all.

Yes, I said it. You can choose to NOT respond.

You don't owe an explanation for what you're feeling. It's okay to choose to not have that conversation. This is especially true when you know it will test your mental and emotional wellness, which is no less important than anyone else's.

Engaging in explanations to manage the emotions of another person at the expense of your own peace is not required of you. You can stop that, right now.

I'm going to say it again: your mental and emotional health is no less important than that of another person. You do not have to sacrifice your peace to 'make' someone feel better. They mostly want you to justify yourself so they can deflect back onto you rather than doing their own work to sort through their own shit. And by playing into it and accepting that deflection, you're not doing them any favors.

You see, the flip side of your disengagement is that you give other people the time and space they need to take responsibility for their emotions. They get to do their work, if they choose. Other people are responsible for their feelings and emotions just like you are responsible for your own.

You cannot 'make' anyone feel anything.

You are not responsible for how they respond to your words and actions. That's their responsibility. And by carrying the weight and burden of their emotions, you are robbing them of the opportunity to stand in their personal power. And that's energetic criminality. So, stop it. Stop taking responsibility for what isn't yours to bear.

I firmly believe our souls chose this existence to experience limitations and learn certain lessons that aren't possible in the spirit realm. We are not humans with a soul. We are souls in this vessel we call human. Given that, a big part of our purpose is to learn those lessons, and part of that is taking responsibility for our emotions and resulting actions. So, when I was taking on the responsibility for the choices my ex made to shield him from the consequences, I was stealing his opportunity to learn. I really was doing him a huge disservice.

That doesn't mean go around and be an asshole to hurt people intentionally, or to use the truth as a hurtful weapon. After all, you will get back what you put out and you're not a sociopath. I find I avoid speaking my intuitive truth for fear of hurting someone's feelings, especially someone who is very dear to me. Sometimes I know there will be fallout and I don't have the energetic bandwidth to handle it in the moment. So I keep my insights to myself.

What I'm really doing by not speaking my truth is robbing the other person of the lesson meant for them. In each interaction, there is an opportunity to learn, and by holding back, I'm withholding an opportunity from them. I'm learning to choose my words intentionally, from a place of love and empathy to help guide the other person to witness the lesson meant for them. I'm not saying I know what that lesson is. When I follow my intuition and the messages I receive, it will be exactly what my counterpart needs in that moment.

Let your intuition guide you to speak your truth. Know that when it's coming from your heart, it will be the right message, at the right time, precisely as it's needed. When you speak your intuitive truth from your heart with love, your words are energetically true, and the message is exactly what you need at the moment. Although people may not feel or receive it in that way, they will eventually perceive it in that light with reflection. When you are connected to your intuitive truth and speak with love, the message is not of you, it is through you. The energy is flowing from source, consciousness, universe, whatever, using you as the conduit and putting that truth into the world.

I experience this specifically in those moments when a certain person keeps coming into my thoughts. Whenever I act on my intuition and send a message telling them they're amazing and loved, that person has needed to hear it, in that moment. Every. Single. Time.

In my case, I learned to speak my truth. I offered an opportunity for those on the receiving end to make an intentional choice and, in the process, learn the lessons meant for them. This meant not making excuses for my ex when he got drunk, or acted inappropriately toward other people. Or when he failed to follow through on a promise and let others down. I stopped doing for him what he could do for himself. And in that simple act of disengagement, I gave him an opportunity to own his personal power, even if he didn't see it that way. That's what it was, a gift for him to take responsibility for his actions and take back his power.

By making excuses and covering the truth, I was not just enabling him to spiral deeper into his addiction. I was robbing him of the opportunity to find his truth and own his power. In my codependent attempt to 'help', I was actually causing more harm to everyone. Once I saw that truth and coupled it with my soul work, it became much easier for me to speak my truth without the emotional attachment and judgment. Doing this helped me to distance further from the entanglement I felt in that relationship.

Looking back, I see that relationship was my opportunity to learn my lessons in this reality.

Ten years. Like I said, I'm a slow learner!

Toward the end of the relationship, as I was making changes and learning those lessons, I felt it. I knew in my soul the manipulative, narcissistic rhetoric I was buying into all those years was bullshit. And that I was, in fact, lovable and deserved better AND that there were people who would love me in the world.

Truth be told, there were already so many people in the world who loved me, but I just couldn't see it because I didn't love myself yet. It's what I needed to learn about life and myself to prepare for healthy relationships with myself and other people.

The final nail in the coffin of that relationship came when I took a class at a Women's Business Development Center. It focused on building a business that aligned with my soul. There I met a core group of people who were each on their own journeys in building their authentic, soul-aligned businesses and we clicked.

After that three-session workshop-style class was over, we continued to meet with a facilitator every other week for a year or two. This group helped me discover the concept of owning my authenticity. I mean, unapologetically OWNING who I am, what I want, and what I believe. It was pivotal in helping me to speak my truth.

But my first challenge was to recognize my authentic self, as I had no idea who I really was down deep. I knew who others expected me to be and who I pretended to be. But I didn't really know who I was. In some ways, I took that opportunity to reinvent myself.

What I knew for sure was this. I didn't like my current iteration and definitely didn't respect her. Most importantly, I didn't want to be her anymore. I wanted more. The real deal. For the first time in my life, it excited me to discover who I was. For real!

I spent the next two years working through my shit. There was A LOT! And I certainly didn't get through all of it.

I recognized how my inauthentic existence was playing out in all of my relationships. And it was not just the romantic one, but also with my family, friends, and business colleagues. By not being authentic, I wasn't fully living and was missing out on all the richness life was offering. I was also depriving the world of my truth and energy by playing small and scared.

Over those years, I figured out how to stop playing an inauthentic role and step outside of the situation to see it from a more neutral perspective. I worked on identifying and processing my emotions and, as I did, I found it came to me more naturally and took less time for me to understand myself. I was able to get to the root cause of my feelings so I could process them and choose an intentional response rather than an unintentional reaction. You want to talk about empowering! I started to feel good about myself. I felt a sense of control rather than flying off the handle, then regretting my words and actions.

Don't get me wrong, I still have a temper, especially in the face of injustice. And my Zen is tested on the regular, but I tend to function from a state of peace and calm rather than a sudden, unintentional reaction to emotion.

One super effective technique when I catch myself in the midst of negative self-talk is to pause and ask, "What would you say to your best friend in this situation?"

Stepping outside of my situation and reframing from a place of empathy has helped me to stop expecting perfection and to give myself some grace. Kindness isn't just for other people. It's for me, too.

At this point, you might wonder what happened to my ex. Well, I can honestly say that leaving him wasn't just the best thing for me, it was the best thing I did for him. It was a clean break. I left and never looked back. I refused all contact with him. The small, simple act of ignoring his calls felt so empowering to me after being at his beck and call for so long.

Mutual friends, and even his parents, tried to plead his case to me. "He's doing so much better. He's really getting his life together. You should give him a second chance."

All the blah, blah, blahs absolutely clarified to me that the greatest gift I gave to him was to stop enabling his behavior. After I left, he took responsibility for his actions and got his shit together. Had I stayed around and continued to make excuses, he would have continued to spiral deeper into his addictions.

STEP UP AND OWN YOUR POWER

What they say is true, you cannot go back. Things change, you evolve and there is no going back—why would you want to?

I didn't need a repeat to learn my lessons—I finally got it! I had given him so many chances and he burned through them one by one.

It felt like all the conversations with friends and family were a cosmic test from the Universe, offering me the option of going back to what was familiar. It was painfully obvious that it was over, and I spoke that truth to all of them.

This was my first genuine opportunity to speak my truth and wield my personal power. At first, I felt so uneasy with a queasy knot in my stomach. But I made myself be true to what I finally knew—who I was, what I wanted, and what I would and would not accept. I felt powerful holding my ground and refusing to be pushed into doing something I knew wasn't right for me. There was no going back. And they were each very surprised. They had always known me to go with the flow and not rock the boat. They seriously thought they could convince me and that I'd backslide into old patterns playing my part. Let's just say I rocked their boats! And I felt good doing it!

So, you may wonder if I have regrets about taking ten years to come to my senses. 'Wasting' so much time in an unhealthy, toxic relationship and allowing myself to be beat down by my choices. That's what most people ask me when I talk about my journey.

The answer: No, not a single regret.

Yeah, it would have been great to figure all my shit out sooner and not 'waste' so much time.

When I look at who I am today and where I am in this moment, knowing that those experiences brought me to this point makes it all worthwhile. You see, I'm completely convinced that all that turmoil and soul searching gifted me with the lessons I needed to be ready for the loving, healthy, supportive relationship I'm in today. I needed to face my insecurity and embrace my authenticity to be ready to accept the intense love and respect my husband gives me every single day.

I know we'll be together forever because all the best couples have a great origin story. Ours is my favorite, and yes, I'm biased.

My husband and I met in college. He was in a band with my roommates and I was a smitten kitten from day one. I had such a crush! I still feel butterflies when I think back to our college days. As I write this, a grin of giddy excitement appears on my face.

After two semesters of running in the same circles and hanging out, I graduated, and we went our separate ways. Only to reconnect sixteen years later via Facebook.

If you ever question the purpose of Facebook, it was so Andy and I could reconnect. Only reason it exists, in my opinion! I knew the moment I peeked out the window and saw him standing on my front porch that he was the one. He had always been the one!

We talked for hours that night and were both completely open. We talked about every aspect of our lives, including our horrifically toxic relationships. Let's just say I'm not the only one who had stuff to work through and lessons to learn during that sixteen year hiatus. That conversation was so comfortable. It was so easy to share my feelings with him. And that was the rekindling that led to our epic love story.

We joke now that had we tried to be together in college, I would have been his first crazy girlfriend instead of his last crazy girlfriend. We speak often about how grateful we are for the time it gifted us to learn what we needed to prepare for what we have now. Our story is a perfect example of 'divine timing'.

Being in an emotionally healthy relationship where I feel safe, respected, and protected is what I deserve. It's what every person deserves. I no longer need to be on high alert to protect myself because I know my husband has my back, and I have his. We are a team, on the same side and we can disagree without judgment and reach a compromise. Truthfully, we are so much on the same page we almost never disagree—except about pineapple on pizza. That's just wrong.

When I look at us, I see a completely harmonious and symbiotic relationship. And, yes, I think we're a big deal! We are each our authentic selves yet come together in a synergistic partnership that continues to deepen and grow.

This is what I want for you.

To recap, this is what works for me. I say 'works' because I'm still on this journey.

◊ Embrace your Personal Power by taking responsibility for your emotions. Disengage when you need time to sort and process your feelings. Then choose an informed response to the situation at hand with full understanding of WHY you're feeling what you feel.

◊ Stop taking responsibility for what is not yours. Allow others the gift of learning the lessons meant for them. Give them the opportunity to take responsibility for their feelings and embrace their Personal Power.

◊ Live Authentically. And do it without apology. You have unique and precious gifts that this world needs. Living as your authentic self and sharing your talents with this world is why you are here.

◊ Follow your intuition. Deepen your connection to that still, small voice. Trust that what flows through your intuition to you is the truth needed in the moment. Then speak that truth from the love in your heart. The message will always be what you need.

◊ Ask yourself:

Who Am I?
What Do I Want?
What Is My Purpose?

◊ Find modalities to help you answer these questions.

My favorite tools to investigate answers to these questions include:

Chakra energy attunement, meditation, visualization, essential oils, and sound healing to maintain a harmonious energy flow for body, mind, and soul.

Numerology has also been an important modality. I have been able to gain insights into understanding myself, my gifts, talents, and potential. Based on just my birthdate, I have a deeper awareness of why I process as I do and how I can shift toward my highest potential. Numerology is also helpful to understand how the Universal energy we are all feeling shows up for me personally. This helps me to understand myself and those around me to improve communication in all my relationships.

I truly believe every person deserves to feel seen, supported, and heard. For each person to feel safe speaking their personal, authentic truth from the heart with love. Imagine a world where each person owned their emotions and instead of blind reaction made cognizant, intentional choices of action.

If we move through this world, heart first, in our personal authentic truth, our experience will shift into a reality of harmony and love.

ABOUT KATRINA LAFLIN, AUTHOR

I'm Katrina and I'm a certified numerologist, an expert energy guide, and wedding officiant on a mission to help you understand who you are and what you want for deeper connections to yourself and in your relationships.

Numerology is my favorite tool to help you understand how your personal energies interact and are influenced by the collective Universal energies experienced by everyone. I use Chakra Alignment techniques to balance your energetic vibrations and harmonize your flow of energy. And I encourage a Low-Toxin Lifestyle to empower energy flow in your physical environment. This threefold approach provides a pathway to manifest a Radically Authentic Life.

After decades of soul searching and personal development to find the pieces I was missing, this holistic approach to the good ol' mind-body-soul concept opened doors to a whole new world of understanding. The transformation I feel incorporating the energy of the numbers into my daily life is tremendous! Taking moments throughout my day to check in with my energy and pace my chakra movement brings a sense of ease. And cleaning up my physical surroundings has manifested improved health and wellness I never knew possible. All of that brought me to embrace my own Radical Authenticity. I call it my SoulScape.

And I want that for you too! I'm here to help you find your true identity, align with your highest potential, and live a life that resonates with your authentic self.

You can reach me through my website and email:

Website: livingyoursoulscape.com
Email: createyoursoulscape@gmail.com

THE POWER OF LANGUAGE
AND THE MEANING YOU GIVE IT
BY SARAH HOLMES

Are you ready to open your perception and expand your awareness and growth through your language?

Language has always fascinated me. This chapter will guide you to notice and make powerful changes to your language from your awareness to your empowered state. It's designed to open spaces in your body, mind, spirit, and heart that have been unplugged and disconnected. As I share my insights and experiences for reflection, it is my wish that you hear, feel, and connect to yourself more deeply. It is my deepest wish for this chapter to nurture and support you in a way that is for your journey and whatever you seek to experience in your life.

As you begin, I encourage you to breathe deeply through the nose and release through the mouth. Do this three times slowly to bring your mind and body into the heart space.

Let's journey together to discover what language you are using, and bring awareness to what you are internally and externally saying to yourself or others. How is your body receiving the vibration of the words, and what meaning have you attached to it? The cells in your body and your heart rewire themselves to reflect your outer world.

Bring awareness to how the body is reacting. Is it tight? Stuck? Sore? Inflexible? Breathe more deeply into the areas where that might be.

I have been a seeker of all kinds of knowledge and truths in many areas of my life to make sense of my life. Why I am here. Who I am in this time and space on Earth. Another way to say it, in this lifetime, but one area in particular, has been how we use, speak, and put meaning to our language for many years and why that is.

I'm not an academic by any means, but I have always listened to the vibration and watched the behaviour of others as they would speak their words and the movements in their body through their own experiences. This led to cultivating my skills to understand what other humans were really saying or even wanting to say and noticing how my body felt during my own exploration with what was I feeling, what was my truth, and what was I not really saying. This awareness had me in deep thought and curiosity with my own external and internal language.

Now I can see it was self-abuse. I'm not saying either of us is an abuser, but we do abuse ourselves with our own language and allow others to as well. In the Oxford Dictionary the word *Abuse* means: *Use (something) to bad effect or for a purpose misuse or treat with cruelty or violence, especially regularly or repeatedly.*

This constant abusive self-talk is really self-abuse. Allow this to land if this is the first time you are hearing this, and notice your body and how it feels.

THE POWER OF LANGUAGE

Ask yourself what your belief is around this subject. Try this. Write it down and see what language you have been programmed with. Yes, programmed and given a belief. You weren't birthed into this world wired with the belief you were not good enough or worthy enough. The meaning behind the last statement can have an impact if the meaning, programming, and belief are drummed into someone enough. It's from a place of lack, which is a belief passed down through generations. (No blame here, just awareness being offered.)

A common theme I see in my experience and through working with clients is that language, meaning, and beliefs have been playing out in repeated patterns. For example, one's disempowering relationship with money has kept them in a place of lack and confusion around money.

Money is energy, and loves to play and create. A nice quote to put on your mirror.

Limiting language, beliefs, and meaning have stopped its flow.

Language, such as the following as a small example, leads to doubt in one's creation.

"I can't possibly be successful and have money."

"I can't have abundance."

"Why didn't XYZ sell?"

"Others need it more than me."

"I lost so much money."

"Money never comes to me."

BEYOND THE SHIFT

Here are changes in the vibration to the examples:

"It is so possible to be successful and have money flowing to me."

"Abundance is always flowing to me and through me."

"My XYZ is worthy of being seen by all."

"I am worthy of all I desire and so are others."

"I am open to the return of my abundance."

"Money loves to come play with me, it loves to flow through me."

I'm here to tell you that money is a good thing and is not to be feared. It's waiting for you to play and does not discriminate. It wants to create and can come into your life in many different forms, not just dollars in your bank account. The art is to release it from the energy and vibration of lack. Be willing to let the money flow and trust in it before you see the physical.

I'm talking about money in these examples, but this language can appear in all experiences. Experiment with it.

It's all about energy and vibration from within and is the meaning that you are driving the language with.

Here are some other replacements:

"Money, I love all the experiences we are having."

"It's such fun to have you flow into and through my life."

"I am getting better at loving myself in all experiences."

THE POWER OF LANGUAGE

This powerful saying from the Hopi Elders Prophecy is an incredible recipe to add to your core intention: "If you want to find the secrets to the universe, think in terms of energy, frequency, and vibration."

While this chapter just touches the surface on this subject of language, my personal stories and tools are intended to help you reflect, ponder, and deepen your understanding. And to become curious, explore the language, beliefs, and meaning you use and ask why.

For example, I'm curious why we say things like "Skin Heads on a Raft". In London terms it means 'Baked Beans on Toast'. My mother always said that term. Or 'money doesn't grow on trees' (which, in essence, it does in its physical form). The meaning behind this was that there wasn't enough which also did mean to me that I was not enough to have it come and create in my life. It formed the thought, *It's for them and not me*. It created a belief that wasn't really mine.

Growing up in London with a single Mum and my brother, I remember feeling so sad inside. I never knew why, at such a young age, I had this internal dialogue that said, "I was not good," or "I'm unable to learn," or "Why am I here? What am I doing here in this school setting?"

I didn't understand and I couldn't ask why, as I felt I didn't have a voice of my own. I wasn't taught the language to express my unique self. Rather others told me to be quiet, and I felt I didn't add any value. I never felt as though I fit in, and whispers inside told me something, but what? I didn't know. It was so confusing trying to hear me and others.

Everything I knew I had been told or shown. How to do this, how this should be done, this is how we always do it. I didn't even know how to question a caregiver about how I felt about information given to me. Was it even my truth? I felt I could never disagree or allow my opinion to be heard. Caregivers didn't nurture how I saw my world through my eyes. I can reflect on it and see that now. I didn't have the language. But I also didn't have the nurturing or guidance to explore what my truth is. What my perception is.

How did you or I know what the truth is without guidance? How do you manage or even express what you're feeling when your caregivers never taught you? Why? Because no one ever taught them. Others programmed into them the meaning and language that was understood by them and passed on as truth.

TV became our new guide. Growing up, I didn't have the tools to connect me to my true essence and abilities. Now, no blame here as my Mum didn't know either, as this was a generational thing. Love you, Mum. xx

As I grew—well, stumbled through my challenges and experiences of life—I cultivated this deep connection with failure and fear, which became my norm. I didn't know why.

If I questioned something for my own deeper understanding, I was challenged by my caregivers' own traumas and misuse of language guidance. They criticised me when I wanted to explore my creative side. What that taught me about adults was that others are more powerful than I am. After all, they are bigger than me, more experienced, right?

THE POWER OF LANGUAGE

Expression was suppressed, shamed, and looked down upon.

I must be wrong in the way I want to think and feel. This kind of thinking fuels the belief that I don't belong.

Oh my, that word, 'belong'. So powerful in its isolation. What do we do? We adjust! Conform and bury our essence. Until we meet like-minded people who gently and softly open our hearts. In our quest to 'find ourselves' we learn to unravel the old language, beliefs, and meaning.

What a journey! I love it.

The truth is, you belong, always have, and always will.

I have this memory of visiting my grandparents, and after completing a simple picture, I signed it 'kolored by Sarah Jane'.

They immediately laughed at me, and the words my grand-parents spoke to each other and then directly to me for spelling it wrong hurt me deeply.

In that moment, the power of language and the meaning they spoke embodied my tiny body with low vibrations of fear, shame, and embarrassment. It made me sink so low that I never wanted to colour again.

Who else would they tell? My Mum? What would she do then? The fear was huge, and more shame was about to swallow me.

They said, "Look she can't even spell."

I quickly threw the picture away and was in a place (unknown to me at the time as I was so little) that I created as protection. I would visit frequently for the remaining younger, teen, and early adult years, which I called the dark wishing well. This was a place where nobody could find me, and it developed into a cave. It was where I would internally go to hibernate, create stories, and allow the playing out of the internal language to create havoc. This led to relationship after relationship that would remind me of all this chaos of disempowerment. They must be right, I would think.

There you have it. The power of language had painted a stroke of colour on me that took years to change back in alignment with my essence, which is so colourful and vibrant today.

Sometimes, when the cave appears, I have ventured into it but never stayed long. It's an ongoing journey through experiences. Someone wise said, "Life's experiences are the dynamics for opportunities for you to choose love and to live life." I now use moments in the cave as opportunities for reflection, self-love, expansion, and growth. It has become a space where it's not dark anymore. It's bright and nurturing.

The above experience caused me to be fearful of writing in front of anyone or sharing my written language. I invented a strategy to prevent myself from being embarrassed or ashamed again. Avoidance was my strategy. I made sure that I would not do anything that involved writing, painting, or having to show anyone anything. So I found things that were practical and was trying to reinvent myself constantly, become a doer, a pleaser, a great avoider.

What did that do for me?

I later found out on my healing journey that it shut down an area of my creativity, and I became a people pleaser with no self-love or trust. I really didn't think I had any help or could amount to much, and I became resigned that this was it. My language and beliefs were supporting me in every direction. I had no idea how to believe in myself and self-expression. My life, aspirations, achievable goals, and desires for what I wanted to experience had become limited instead of limitless. Over time, I had mastered the strategy of avoidance.

I was missing out on life and the growth that comes with mistakes and learning. The power of language had been so meaningful to me.

The self-abuse I was doing was growing.

Can you relate this story to a moment when something similar happened to you? Where you stopped enjoying something or gave it up due to an experience of language, meaning, and belief?

Again, my grandparents' beliefs and actions were not their fault. They were unaware of the powerful meaning given to them and the impact they would have had. They didn't understand how they influenced, concreted, and programmed me and, in essence, shaped me.

It was unconscious behaviour on their behalf. Most operate from the unconscious mind without questioning or awareness of their emotions and behaviours as we have never been taught. In the Oxford Dictionary, the definitions for unconscious are:

1. in a state like sleep because of an injury or illness, and not able to use your senses

2. (of feelings, thoughts, etc.) existing or happening without you realising or being aware; not deliberate or controlled

3. The part of the mind which is inaccessible to the conscious mind but which affects behaviour and emotions.

We store things in the subconscious, and they play out without us fully knowing.

It's generational language and ways that have been passed down from caregivers, teachers, and peers for many years. No one questions anything due to fear, retribution, or punishment. In these current times, we are trying to find peace, our voice within, and to be the best versions we can possibly be. Some people reflect this to others and are of service to humanity.

Self-development and training in modalities have given me a deep understanding of trauma held in the body, mind, and spirit. Self-love has brought awareness to my language, behaviour, and deeper connection to how my body feels. This has led me to my personal power, especially around my Yes's and No's.

A powerful example was when I was a DJ in Greece at 19, which I loved so much. Reflecting on this, I realise I didn't have any power in my language to say No. Nor did I have the ability to ask questions still or hold strong in my own thoughts and beliefs. What developed in my belief system was that I didn't know anything, accompanied by a fear of being told I was stupid.

I was terrified that someone would say, "I can't believe you didn't know that."

I had an inability to simply hear another person's opinions and not put any other meaning to the language they were sharing. I just thought it was all my fault and I was stupid. Would others accept my opinion even if they disagreed? I had no skills in holding energy for others and just kept going with the flow of others and using my avoidance strategy. This came from other people's language and beliefs, which I also accepted and believed in. Ultimately, it became my language. At 19, it was also about body image and how beautiful another person thought you were. One believed they must think that too, but really, it's conditioning or programming instilled in us at an early age.

This story highlights how things get programmed through language.

A young girl aged five is the sparkle of everyone's life. Her family adorns her with patience, presence, love, and attention. The little girl's aunties and uncles, who visit frequently, remind her how loved she is. She would wait at the door, and as they walked in, they would use language, "Oh, you look so pretty today with a bow in your hair and cute dress."

They would squeeze her cheeks with love and kisses.

This went on for many months.

One day, her mother gave birth to her little sibling. She was so excited to meet and welcome the baby and knew she was the big sister now. As usual the aunties and uncles were about to visit, and she wore a pretty dress and a bow in her hair. She opened the door, and they walked in with such urgency and excitement that they barely gave any attention to this young five-year-old.

One by one they came in asking, "Where is the baby? I want to see the baby."

At that moment the little girl has a choice. She can start the internal language of, "What's wrong with my bow? My dress? Me? They don't love me any more or think I'm cute."

Or she can choose, if she is aware, to love herself. If she knows about her emotions, that she IS love and SHE is loved. Then she understands their language is excitement for the new baby, whom she also has deep excitement and love for.

Either way, she put meaning to the language she just heard.

Has your self-abuse language sounded similar to these statements?

"I'm so silly."
"I'm so stupid (even stated in a slightly humourous way)."
"I am not good at this."
"I'm ugly."

"That's for others and not me."

"Nothing ever happens for me that good."

If so, it's deeply connected to the meaning we give to our language that has been received through experiences and programming. This is something we have learnt in our subconscious and then practised from a young age.

One of my mentors, Brad, used to say, "**Practise Makes Permanent**". How accurate is this statement for both sides of the coin?

These language patterns follow us through the stages of life.

For me, these patterns continued as a mother of three beautiful, incredible children, my most significant teachers of all time, space, and dimensions.

They taught me a lot when my internal dialogue got loud, and becoming a parent amplified it. Children reaffirm and reflect this within you. The things you have avoided or suppressed show up in the children's needs, their emotions, expression, understanding, their Yes's and No's. And as we go through growth and stages of life, it starts to show up in other areas.

I hope you see the tapestry in language, beliefs, and programming. And how it threads through every aspect of your life and all you interact with. Every one of us has had our own conditioning, programming, and beliefs in the system of language. It starts to develop and bring in more meaning and new language as we see how this is passed down through our generations.

BEYOND THE SHIFT

The language it now develops into can create triggers and judgements. It can come from other experiences such as:

Our first relationship. Our first job. Our bosses.
Our siblings. Family members. Friendships. Children.
Pets. Husband. Wife. Parents. Strangers.
Our inability to balance emotions in a social setting.

The tapestry is extensive.

So you see, we are not alone in the inner landscape of language, as everyone has been told similar stories and narratives. Each of us has unique experiences and meanings we put to it, and then we all come together trying to figure it out. It's called life. When we know this, we can start to bring in more compassion, more self love, more patience. We start understanding and seeing through the veil of our own truths.

By the time I was in my 40s, I had established this internal language that I wasn't good at math. Many people had told me that through different stages of my life, so it became my belief. When someone asked me a question about numbers, I would automatically say, "Oh, I'm rubbish at numbers."

I'd bring in the learned strategy I had when I was 10, which was to avoid it at all costs. How can I please them and be practical to cover up my shame?

At this stage, my kids were seeking me out for guidance. I could do the basics with them, but I was all over the place with anything complicated when they entered high school.

THE POWER OF LANGUAGE

My strategy was to say, "Ask your father. Can I make you a sandwich?" Practical avoidance.

One day, I decided enough was enough, and I would see how bad I really was. So I signed up for a mathematics course, and my heart raced when the first question while filling out the application was 'What level'?

My strategy mind, the language I had befriended, was going crazy, almost screaming, *STOP, shut it down!* I was able to override the pattern, and I kept going as I was also doing this for my kids.

It came time for my first lesson online. I had sweaty palms, my heart was racing, and I was in a 'flight' response. When you are triggered, you are apt to have a fight, flight, freeze, or faint response. I was ready to flee.

A lovely 23-year-old university student greeted me.

I was terrified.

She asked, "Where do you want to start?"

With tears swelling, I said, "From the very beginning."

And with those words came shame, and I burst into tears. This young girl held space and said, "That's okay. Let's see what you know and go from there."

It took all my strength to not close my laptop down, and I mean ALL MY STRENGTH. With that first lesson out of the way, I continued with her for six months.

BEYOND THE SHIFT

My instructor showed me I wasn't that bad after all, and I loved numbers. Most of it wasn't necessary for my purpose in life and what I wanted to create. I concentrated on what I connected to and how that would support me in my up-and-coming property business adventure. Now, I had the confidence to lean into the understanding that I don't know it all and won't use it all. I could now ask for help and feel the strategy that I had held for so long start to dissolve.

I learnt that making 'mistakes' (which really are not mistakes) is not a bad thing, and I became more comfortable with my language and expression. It made shifts in many areas of my life, and I was so happy with myself.

I got to a point where I said to myself, *I feel complete and happy with the knowledge.*

This became my mantra in the future whenever there was something that was not where my energy needed to be. Or, not feeling fear, I would ask another person to explain it to me.

If I need to know something that I want to re-visit, I have the power and the capacity to ask. I can see life opening up.

I had finally released, with gratitude and love, a pattern of language that had power over me. That I had given power to for far too long.

So you see, I share these personal stories with the wish you can relate to and ponder your own stories on your journey. I hope you can see and claim your power in your language and meaning. And believe in your ability to open up to the experiences you wish to have (or close the door on) with courage, strength, and guidance.

We are not meant to travel through this growing awareness within ourselves alone. We are Source energy, the God energy with whom you choose. Our essence created us, and we are born innocent and pure. And, as children, we are meant to experience all that life has for us to expand, learn, and grow. We grow into our purpose.

Languages are a way for us to communicate.

Over time, scholars and leaders decided to change, alter, and give language different meanings which we now use. They got passed down through many generations, and we are now realising the original meanings intended through language.

Acknowledging all the mentors who helped me along my journey is important. The guidance was more than just professional. Mentors also gave me the insights to understand my thoughts, language, and meaning that had caused me to suffer in my own self-abuse—where I was giving my power away to things I was 'supposed' to value. They helped me to see my worth and to reflect deeper love for who I am, what my truth is, and what my beliefs, values, and worth are for me. I could see how the patterns of my language and meaning had been holding me back, and all that had taken place was just perfect to bring me to where I am and who I am today.

Let's go deeper into awareness with some science about how language affects our physical bodies. As a body worker in the field of Biodynamic Cranial Sacral, it was clear that internal abuse was causing disease. It was an energy that was not heard or seen to manifest into physical. Having this awareness on a deep level is so empowering and has the power to change you.

I have to be clear in this statement that it is not to get rid of, nor a cure, but rather a state of being with no matter. I have seen things move and shift when clients' perceptions, language, and awareness change.

Can you see how your experiences can alter your perception, your meaning, and mould you through no fault of your own or others? No one taught you, or gave you any awareness at school, either.

We have already dove into the less empowering programming of language and how this can, and may still, be impacting you. Mentally, physically, and spiritually.

Your **external voice** also influences you. You are the first to hear the words you speak. Your physical body and other people then receive your words. And the cycle continues.

Your internal language is a result of your outer world experiences. What you see and experience is directly related to your internal state and your external language which are the same thing, really.

Let's see how you can make small changes to empower you in the way you use your internal language and spoken language. I have found this wisdom and these methods worked for myself and my clients.

THE POWER OF LANGUAGE

Here are two questions to ask yourself:

1. How many times have you told yourself you are not good enough? Really think about this.

   If you want to take it further just for giggles, please grab a pen and paper.

   a. Draw a line down the centre of the page.

   b. Write on one side the things you say lovingly to yourself daily.

   c. On the other side, the things you say that are not loving.

   d. See what you notice. Write your awarenesses.

   Whatever you wrote, I assure you that you are enough and always have been. You are on an incredible journey of the I AM.

2. Can you let this be your truth?

   Now that you have a mental or physical list, put that paper aside, as we will return to it.

Let's dive into the **science of language**.

Have you heard about the book by the author Masaru Emoto, "The Hidden Messages in Water"?

Dr. Emoto's studies revealed that what we say in our tone and frequency has a significant effect on water. He collected different water samples from around the world and started the experiments.

Here's what happened with the water taken from very polluted parts of the world. First, he froze the water and viewed the structure under a powerful microscope. The images were what I would call unhealthy, sad, and not alive. He then used prayer words over the water every day over a period of time. His results showed that the structure of the water changed into a noticeable snowflake—a healthier, happier, more vibrant-looking pattern.

During another study, he played heavy metal music, and the water could not make a snowflake. The pictures of water in his book looked confused and unhappy. It's fascinating research, and I highly recommend his book if you haven't read it.

There are many stories of experiments where people speak to plants with similar results. When they use disempowering dialogue, the plants wilt, turn away, and often die. The language that caused this were statements such as:

"You're so useless."
"Why do you bother?"
"I hate you."

They noticed the water turned a very unhealthy colour and lost its vibrancy. Its life force broke down.

When people speak to plants using loving language, they lean towards where the person's energy comes from, blossoming. Language such as the following helps plants to grow and expand their vibrant life force.

"Oh, you're so wonderful."
"You make me smile."

THE POWER OF LANGUAGE

"I love how you are always growing and doing your best."
"I love you so much."
"I can see how you are growing into your purpose."

The reason I am sharing this is because we are 80% water. Think about this. If we are 80% water (give or take), then surely what and how we speak, what we listen to, matter. They have the ability to change our molecular structure.

When I got this at a cellular level, I realised that our language and the words we speak and think matter. My belief matters, and I matter. I am worthy of all the divine love, and I allow more love to flow within and through me. And the same is true for you.

Our entire world is made of frequency and vibration (which is why we are one) that we have manifested through our language and words. Or did they manifest language and words? (Oh, the age-old question, which came first, the chicken or the egg?)

These inquiries were so cool. They led me down a wonderful path of self-awareness and now my life's work shows up in my purpose every day. And I am always doing my best in all experiences.

What came next was a deeper awareness.

We have put many meanings to our language and given it so much power. It can either bring us to our knees in suffering or elevate us into LOVE.

Let's look at an example. Think of a tree.

In the English language, we call it a Tree, although in another language, it will be called something different, but the meaning will be the same. This allows us to understand each other and communicate what we need.

I have noticed that the Tree has now become described in language and has meaning put to it (remember, language is also judgement) as a thin tree, a fat tree, or even an ugly tree.

This is a simple explanation to illustrate how the power of our language has gained strength and been used to keep us small, contained, and controlled. Think about other ways this could also be true.

This is even used by really awesome parents who tell their kids Santa Claus exists. This was not just for fun, but it was unconscious. It became a bargaining tool we did not understand as a kid and gave away our power of expression. It suppressed emotions, even deeply expressed emotions, which we didn't understand for fear of Santa Claus not arriving with the gifts we wanted. Again, it's no one's fault—it's ancestral, a generational narrative of control passed down from generation to generation.

Here's the bubble burster.

The reason behind their actions was to make themselves feel better by making us behave a certain way.

It was a kind of bargaining tool, as they were going through their own stuff of not understanding their own emotions. It was a learned way to bring control over another. (Yes, I did it too, until I became aware.) They could not cope with their own emotions.

There you have it.

Santa is just one example, but it's universal in most cultures.

I'm sorry if you still believe in Santa, but let's make him a nice guy. Someone who is about the gift of giving and the coming together of communities and souls.

What I'm saying isn't law and is my opinion. It's my perspective and understanding through my experiences. I'm using these reflections to help guide you to your own understanding of the power of your language. It has helped me come out of suffering and into a more loving, compassionate way of living. Let's allow ourselves and our children to feel, express, and gift ourselves a great guide for parenting. It is a path to change how we empower future generations to become more self-empowered human beings.

MAKE NEW CHOICES. ASK QUESTIONS.

Be curious, and don't let fear run the show.

So once we realise Santa is not real, we do not necessarily know how to step into our power and manage our emotions. This is huge as a child. We don't realise we can step out of the program. So, we spend many years working on all our suppressed emotions and what we didn't do because of something that didn't exist.

The best news is that you have the ability to change it.

BEYOND THE SHIFT

You can start the unravelling, by first bringing in awareness of your own internal language. This influences the outer voice and inner voice, which then changes the molecular structure of the water in your body to be a more loving, kind being to yourself. This will show up in your reality—your outer world of experiences.

We are the voice of love.

I will share with you some tools that have helped me change how I speak to myself through internal dialogue.

Let's return to that piece of paper and pen I asked you to put aside earlier.

Seeing the power of language on paper can bring an awareness of language. We think we're thinking, but we're not. We're programming ourselves. Thinking differs significantly from programming, which happens at a subconscious level.

Thinking is clarity.

Got that list?

a. Notice the words of your internal language you say regularly that are not for your highest good.

b. List them all. Go for it. Once this is done, do it on the other side for the loving, kind things you say about yourself. They might include messages like, "I love my body. I love me."

c. Once you have done this, do you notice if you have more empowering or disempowering words of language?

d. Which did you find easier to write?

I invite you to ask yourself why.

Earlier, you learnt the meaning you gave them and perfected it into being permanent. Just allow yourself to acknowledge the awareness you now have about what you have been saying repeatedly to yourself. YOU CAN'T UNDO THE AWARENESS. Rewire your brain. Choose to accept you. Love you, and choose you in every moment. Can you give it a meaning that is supportive, loving, and kind?

We want to shift beyond the language that doesn't serve you and your highest good.

You do this moment by moment, experience by experience—one awareness at a time.

You're doing great.

Next, let's have a look at a tool with **sound healing**.

The healing sounds of nature are a wonderful way to bring love into your heart space to feel your essence and your body of water that lives inside you.

Have you ever had a sound-healing bath?

It's a wonderful way to bring in a frequency and vibration to the water body and all its other structures.

Most bowls carry the sound of each chakra, although some are universal sounds.

There have been many studies around sound, and some studies show it through a vibration frequency. You can find music with Earth's frequency of 7.83hz on Spotify or other platforms.

Frequency is the number of occurrences of a repeating event per unit of time. I use different ones to help me concentrate and relax. You can find ones for anything you wish. I am playing one as I write to bring inspiration, which I play in the background. There are ones for cleansing your home, too.

You can easily search online to find more research. And, if you have yet to experience a sound bath, pop it on your bucket list.

You can find a frequency in a song that touches your heart. It can induce emotions of happiness, sadness that may want to arise, or even grief. Listening to songs is a tool I like to use. If I am studying or looking for Sunday Café vibes, I will look for those types of songs.

The trick here is to feel with your inner power of awareness. How do you feel when you listen to a song or attend a sound bath?

This becomes about you recognising your language from your inner world to your outer world and actually believing in it. Seeing changes you desire, visualising how you desire to see every experience, and creating new meanings that are your truth. When you do this you are creating the life you desire and the universe wishes to create with you.

What is your response when someone gives you a compliment like, "You look beautiful"?

The response you're listening for is not from them first but from yourself. It happens in a nanosecond. I bet you say something along the lines, "Oh, so do you." or "Oh, not really, not me." Or when you are given a gift, your response is, "Oh, you shouldn't have." This is a reflection of not being able to receive. How cool would it be if you responded with, "Thank you, that's so loving and kind of you."? Try this next time.

Another tool is to create a list of wonderful, meaningful songs that bring joy and uplift you.

The Imaginary Wand

Now that you have this awareness, there is another tool I like to use, which is so much fun. It requires you to use your amazing creative imagination. So think childlike. This Imaginary Wand lives within you, and you get to place it anywhere within you. Your back. Your heart. It's totally your decision. You cannot get this wrong.

Okay, you've created and placed this in your space.

a. Every time you become aware of saying anything on that list of disempowering dialogue, you zap it with your Imaginary Magical Wand.

b. Replace it with an empowering message.

c. See the next page as you will be making a list.

BEYOND THE SHIFT

I like to have mine form butterflies in the zapping, as they're a symbol of transmutation.

Please do whatever feels good for you. After each one, take a deep breath and release. This helps and supports the physical body. Replace with a positive affirmation of love.

Another opportunity for zapping:

a. When someone gives you a compliment, answer with a simple 'Thank you'.

b. And wait. Let it rest in you.

c. If you feel resistance, then zap the resistance with your Magic Wand.

d. Make a list of your new empowered language and read it daily. This will replace those moments you zap the disempowered ones.

e. Place them on sticky notes or your phone as an alert to go off at a certain time. I like numbers, so 11:11 am is a good time for me to schedule an alert.

f. Write something empowering that resonates.

Here are my examples:

"Today is a beautiful day, and you are glowing with love and light."
"I love you so much."
"I am getting better every day."
"I am always doing my best in any given moment."
"I have the ability to figure things out."

Oh, my spelling! Well, I appreciate technology and spell check. Even more importantly, I have cultivated my tools with my inner dialogue power to be okay if I spelled a word incorrectly or forgot how it's spelled.

My internal mind state is becoming unbound by my disempowering statements. If I am surprised by one, I simply use my tools above to zap it with my wand and replace it with a kind, loving word.

Here's an ultimate tool for you. It is one of my favourites to hone the power of language. Write **powerful statements in your journal.** A wonderful young man named Jake gifted these to me.

"I am a Powerful Goddess of light."
"I am competent."
"I am capable."
"I step into my power now."

I believe we all have the power within and that we are never broken. Seeking another to assist us in guiding and empowering us on our journey beyond our shift is most helpful. Be the empowered spirit and set your intention to be guided to the right teacher who sees you in all aspects.

In the event of an emergency, go back to the tool that resonated the most with you. The Imaginary Wand is the one I go to the most.

I would like to share these final thoughts as we close this chapter on the power of language.

You are not responsible for how others respond or react to you. What you are responsible for is how you use your language and how you respond to others.

You see, everyone has their own journey, experiences, beliefs, and faiths.

It is up to each one of us to be the best version of ourselves in any moment. An example is when you have a headache. You are still showing up as the best version of yourself. If you have slept all day for whatever reason, you are still showing up as the best version of yourself. No judgement.

One way I respond to my friends and family when they say a disempowering word or phrase about themselves in front of me is to lovingly look at them and say, "Please don't talk to my best friend [my incredible son, my incredible daughter, my mother, my partner] like that. I love them so much."

I found they always received this response in their awareness of choice.

Yes, you've got this. You have a choice in everything you do. I trust you found this content empowering and insightful. I wish you an amazing journey as you also start to light your lantern for all you come into contact with, especially the connection with yourself.

Change starts with you and it will ripple into the outer world that you are creating.

You have begun a wondrous journey of new truths that will forever empower you. I am so proud of you and delighted that you have committed to yourself and to all your ancestors from past and present.

With love, light, and gratitude always,
Sarah Jane

ABOUT SARAH HOLMES, AUTHOR

A little about me and the gratitude I hold for many people.

I am a mother of three incredible children: Tanya, Adam, and Sian. These beings are my greatest gifts.

To my children, I am deeply grateful to you for all you have shown me and the different journeys we have travelled together.

Without you, there cannot be me, for you have shown me all I desired to see and be in this wonderful world.

Through you all I have been able to expand and grow. I love you all deeply. xxx

To my Mother, Brenda, for always being my biggest cheerleader and believing in me. Thank you for being open to all our conversations of healing and honouring our journey in truth that you so courageously are taking to dive deep into your own language dialogue.

To my incredible friends and many more, I have deep gratitude to you all for your wisdom through your own experiences and gentle, loving support in all I do.

I have studied many modalities over the past ten years, which started when my kids were young. I was a Teacher's Aide for children with special needs and moved into Personal Training.

I found I had a gift for holding space and loved being with people and listening to them, holding their perceived suffering as they spoke about their lives and trauma. I impact them by listening deeply to their words, language, and heart, and I help guide them to their inner lantern.

I am grateful to have found a modality called Biodynamic Cranial Sacral, which helps with trauma that is held in the body. I received a Diploma in Biodynamic Cranial Sacral in Sydney, Australia. I am a Certified Meditation teacher, and I studied Basic Numerology, Reiki Mastery, Sound Healing, Quantum Field Dynamics, Spinal Flow, Spinal Energetics, Shamanic Healing, Pleiadian Lightwork Levels 1 & 2, and Holistic Counseling.

This wisdom came through many mentors, as I alluded to earlier: The Ruiz Family, Joy Kingsborough, Brad Cassidy, davidji, and Unplug Meditation.

I loved creating my tool box of modalities over the years as my children were growing.

And now, I have become a contributing published author, which I am honoured to be a part of. Thank you, Pamela Lynch, for your wisdom and belief in my stories and passion, and the invitation to share in this amazing space Beyond The Shift.

ABOUT SARAH HOLMES, AUTHOR

To all the other authors of this book, I love you all so much, and I have deep gratitude for you. We are forever connected in our truth.

To you, the reader, I send you love and light and look forward to the unfolding of your journey.

Love and light,
 Sarah, xxx

You can learn more about Sarah on her website: www.essentialwellnesswithin.com.au

Connect with her on Instagram at: Ewellnesswithin and through e-mail: sjeww@outlook.com

UNFUCK YOURSELF
RELIGIOUS TRAUMA TO SPIRITUAL FREEDOM
BY ANGELA KAYE SIMON

This is a story about my childhood, my soul, and our planet. And this is also a future story about what is coming and why it's time to decide collectively to shift as a planet.

Shift from what? Great question!

Shift away from the collective trauma of religion and dogma and choose to shift beyond that to the new chapter. The good news is that we don't have to ditch spirituality to do it. We just have to shake it out and powerwash the toxicity out of it, and I believe we can do that.

This is an invitation for you to ask if you believe we can and if you are willing to do your part. This is an invitation for you to ask if you're willing to unfuck yourself as we shift beyond religious trauma and into a future of spiritual freedom.

In order to tell the story, we have to talk about why it's important and why it matters.

I knew as a young child I felt the calling to spiritual leadership. And at that time, I imagined I would be a minister because my grandfather was. It is what I knew, and what had been role-modeled as spiritual leadership. As an even younger child, I had seen my first ghost. My mom and grandmother told me it wasn't real, but in my gut, I knew it was. This "knowing," and trusting it, was spiritual leadership, even as a mere child, but we'll talk about that later.

I loved going to church, and it felt special getting to put on the white robe and lighting the candles! Everything about church felt sacred—singing, praising, and worshipping! I loved feeling so connected to the energy of something larger than myself and how natural that came to me. It was incredible seeing other people when they connected to that energy. I loved the way they felt different to me and the way their colors changed.

I was confused when the people who were colorful, lit up, and full of life and beauty at church, talked about the act of seeing spirits like it was evil. Or as if the spirits were evil. I knew the energies I was seeing were not evil, and were not that different from them. The spirits were the same color that the living people were when they were singing and praising at church. I also knew that many of them were people we had sat beside in church in the past but who had crossed. I also didn't think I was evil. And it was confusing, hurtful, and scary as a child to think that if they knew that I could see spirits, they would think that I was!

Spiritually, growing up was confusing for so many reasons. But one thing I knew was, I wanted to be a minister!

Until the day it all changed, and I walked away from the church and swore I would never go back. I did eventually go back, but it took decades and another ten years after that for me to fully heal my relationship. It took time to move beyond the trauma I experienced and the collective trauma I witnessed over many lifetimes. I chose collective healing through spirituality. But, spoiler alert, I am not a minister.

GROWING UP GIFTED

I didn't grow up like other kids did. I grew up poor, rural, in a midwestern farming community in the early 80s and 90s. That part isn't unusual, I suppose. My parents divorced before it was common and accepted (and certainly so in that little village). My mom put herself through school and became a teacher. She volunteered for the Special Olympics, and she brought us along. It was a regular "after-school special," I suppose, at least for those who didn't know what was happening.

Back then, my mom and family didn't know what I was—other than very different. And I tried during my entire childhood to be "normal." The harder I tried to suppress and push it all away, the more the energy flew out in sideways directions and was harder to handle.

That's the thing though, because many inexplicable things happened.

There were the ducks (that we didn't own and never saw) laying eggs at the bottom of the basement stairs for us to find. The cat that just vanished (completely). And the fact that I saw my first spirit when I was a mere five years old.

In kindergarten, I experienced a near-kidnapping experience that my family thought I made up. I was so terrified that I refused to walk to school and needed my mom to arrange for a special bus to pick me up.

Then there was the time I saw a Big Bird that was as tall as the church walking down our street.

When a friend's grandmother passed away at school I sobbed hysterically as if it was my own grandmother, because that's how it felt.

I have clear-as-day memories of events that adults in my family attended and swear I wasn't present for. Yet I can describe them vividly as memories I was present for.

Emergency plans were made, so I had escape routes to get out of my house, because the things I saw were so terrifying that I couldn't sleep. My mom helped me plan out how I would get out of my house if they happened.

And that's just the tip of the iceberg. You see, I grew up gifted—in a very active house.

Looking back, my mom often tells me that she wishes she had understood earlier about energy in the way we do now. And I remind her that she did her best—and she did! I needed to have those experiences in order to know how essential it is to do the work I do now and to share my journey. It gave me the experiences to teach others to step into their own spiritual gifts and to help others shift our world into one where people like me are understood, supported, and celebrated.

As I said, that is a list of inexplicable things that seem odd to many folks. Let's look at that list of things from my childhood again. This time with the eyes of a professional witch and psychic who can define these experiences for you.

The whole duck eggs we found at the bottom of the cellar stairs (with no duck) are evidence of the many portals that were present in my childhood home. (And there are so many stories about these portals, but the eggs stand out to everyone in my family because how bizarre!)

Sure, cats go missing sometimes, but we knew for sure we had not let this cat outside, and we looked EVERYWHERE for this cat, and it was literally never found. It had a vet appointment because it was sick, and we couldn't locate it to bring it to the vet. It was just—gone. Another portal! There are so many portals around us. I learned later in life that I open portals quite naturally (and then learned to close the ones I open and that others open as well).

Seeing the first spirit when I was five is pretty self-explanatory. It is the earliest memory of my mediumship channel being active. And it terrified me. My mom and grandma didn't know how to discuss it with a child, so they told me it wasn't real. I spent the rest of my childhood trying to convince myself it wasn't real and keeping it a secret. Imagine what would happen if we didn't ask our children to suppress their gifts!

The (near) kidnapping experience was the only way I had to interpret a scary experience I had as a child. An experience that was common among many of us who grew up gifted during this time period. And it wasn't unique to where I lived, as there are experiences like these that others share from a variety of countries around the world. Few of us discussed this with anyone other than gifted children like ourselves. Many of us underwent experiences like being followed by vans, aptitude tests, and extra testing at school that other students didn't do. I understand, as an adult, that my brain interpreted it as a threat because it was. (I did not have this knowledge or understanding as a child to explain to the adults in my life.) And I give myself a lot of credit for being able to communicate enough to keep myself safe—even if the adults in my life didn't understand. Imagine if we had had adults who understood us and sought to believe and understand children instead of dismissing their stories. What a powerful world we'd be in.

My psychic abilities have always included feeling the emotions and physical sensations of other people. For this reason, being in school was always extremely difficult for me. When my friend's grandmother died when I was a young child, her grief was excruciating. It was before I understood my mediumship channel and before I had lost anyone close to me. I had never felt grief like that myself. My first time processing and feeling grief was through another human. When I feel emotions (or physical sensations), they come in as if they are my own. And that day, her loss gutted me.

These same abilities, misunderstood by adults, led to a misdiagnosis of emotional impairment when I was in High School. I do not resent that because it also allowed me to remove myself from classes (where I was picking up the emotions of other students) and study in a quiet room alone. Imagine, however, the way we could change things for humans if we stopped pathologizing their spiritual gifts. And instead taught them how they worked and allowed them to be their superpowers!

Growing up, I had the memories of being at multiple events, but the adults around me claimed I hadn't been there. I could explain the entirety of these events and could see them in my mind. For the longest time, this was extraordinarily confusing for me. It is now easy for me to explain having clear-as-day memories of events that I wasn't physically present for.

As an adult, I understand that I astral projected to be present for the events. Imagine living in a world where these things are understood and accepted with the same validity of truth that we accept the facts of gravity. I wonder how many children (or adults, for that matter) are astral-projecting at night and how many are coming back with solutions and cures for world problems, but we dismiss them as "dreams" because we are indoctrinated by dogma.

And the emergency plans that we had because of the visions I had. They were visions. They were premonitions of timelines that were (very) possible. Many of my spiritual gifts came in at a young age, and premonition was one of them. I did not, however, have the word for it until I was much older. Thankfully, my mom helped me come up with escape plans so I could feel more prepared and safe in my body. She didn't understand, and she didn't even believe it was a "real" threat. But she understood it was real for me, and that for me to have peace, I needed a plan for safety. There is real love in that.

If more parents could do this for their children, and more partners could do this for their loved ones, the world would feel safer for a lot more people. As a result, the world would have people who are more happy and secure.

GROWING UP "DIFFERENT"

I grew up gifted, but I didn't know it. I just knew I was different than society told me I was supposed to be. And I knew it disappointed the adults around me, who I wanted nothing more than to make happy and for them to love me. I knew it made me "weird." And the message I got from society and the people in my life, intentionally or unintentionally, was that weird was unlovable.

And the older I got, the more aware I became of how different I was. The more I just wanted to fit in. The more I wanted to have friends or for my siblings to not see me as the weird one. The more it felt like there was a war waging inside of me. A war, where I was learning to hate everything that made me gifted and special, because it also made me different.

Growing up, we're often taught that we need to follow the social norms, follow the rules, and not ruffle feathers. Parents and adults don't teach those things because they are bad people. They teach them to keep us safe.

There is an unspoken social contract in society that rewards those who follow the rules and norms with a generally more happy life. Society reinforces the social pressure to follow the rules and expectations through punishment when we do not follow those rules. Those punishments can be more obvious (in the case of legal ramifications for not following the rules) and less obvious (in the form of social pressure and peer pressure). It causes people to try to "fit in" by following the rules and not "standing out" too much. Chances are you've had some experience in your life where you stepped outside of the common boundaries of society. And outside pressure was used to promptly encourage you to step back in place. Or, when you vented to someone about it, they told you it was your fault because you stepped outside of the boundaries. This is another common way society passively reinforces these social contracts.

SACRIFICING OUR GIFTS FOR "SAMENESS"

The challenge with the expectation that people not be "different" and adhere to norms that expect a certain amount of sameness is that inherently human beings are unique. We know this socially, but we know it all the way down to the makeup of our DNA. We literally are genetically unique from every other human. And by creating a pressure to conform to an artificial sameness, it actually creates the opposite experience for people. By denying our differences and individuality and insisting that we artificially pretend to be similar, we learn that it's not okay to be ourselves. We follow social mores, norms, and rules, and punish those who do not. We teach people to abandon their truth, authenticity, and intuition. And we teach them that to receive things like love and acceptance, they have to bargain with a society that requires this very considerable sacrifice from them.

Furthermore, in this strange experience, in trying to mandate everyone be the "same," we teach people to look for "sameness," and to strive for it. We teach them that sameness is the measure of good, safety, and love. But, people ultimately have to always work to try to fake being the same. So they never actually find the "same" if they are still trying to pretend to be something they aren't.

And in the end, it creates separation, loneliness, and deep sadness. It also creates a society that is deeply afraid of things that differ from what they have been taught is normal, and it creates a society that is ripe for mental health struggles.

REJECTING SAMENESS TO ACCEPT A SOUL MISSION

What I understood pretty early on as a young adult is that sometimes we're the odd duckling because we arrived early to help bring about the change for the world. I understand this much better as I have gotten older.

This is not uncommon. It is common for the "black sheep" or "odd duckling" to actually be the "early adopter," as the tech world would call us. If we look back in history, it's common to hear in the stories of leaders across industries and social movements that they were agitators. They pushed people beyond what was comfortable and asked people to think harder than they were ready to think. Leaders asked questions that made people uncomfortable. They challenged ideas and norms, and even beliefs, that were accepted as fact and truth.

This was true for people like Albert Einstein, Rosa Parks, Martin Luther King Jr, Harvey Milk, Vandana Shiva, Stephen Hawking, Alice Paul, and thousands of others.

It was even true of the spiritual leaders and "ascended masters," like Jesus and Mother Mary when they were in human form and still a person like you and me. Many of the spiritual "greats" were considered "difficult" in their formative years and considered "rebels" by many throughout their lives. All too often, it isn't until after someone has long died and left our earthly world that we understand their wisdom and contributions.

I am not saying I am like Jesus, Einstein, or MLK. But I am saying that, like them, others can misunderstand us when our souls arrive here to help create change and propel society forward. Our presence is not one that is always comfortable for others. And yet, it's essential.

THE FALL OF THE TEMPLE

Along with growing up gifted, I also grew up Christian— well, kind of—until age nine. My paternal grandfather was a minister, and my mother had been raised Catholic. Her father was Catholic, and her mother had never converted but supported her children being raised Catholic. So, I grew up with a strong Christian foundation.

While it might sound strange after everything I just told you about portals, ghosts, and ducks, I felt the calling to be a spiritual leader from the time I was just a young child. Everything about going to church excited me. It felt special to put on the white robe and light the candles! I loved how connected I felt in church, to spirit, and to others. This created a desire to be a minister. It was Christianity that I had as a young child that formed my idea of spiritual leadership. So I assumed, as many do, that if I felt called to spiritual leadership, that it must mean ministry.

Like many who hide behind the power of the church, my grandfather was not the man he pretended to be. There is a long, long, long list of women (and girls) out there who can tell you those stories. Ones that paint the story of a monster better suited for storytelling of a being painted in red, with horns, who lived in a world of fire. And when I was nine years old, I told the truth about my grandfather, and my world changed. That's a story and a book for another day. The important part here is that you understand that in my world, on that day when I was nine years old, the temple crumbled and fell.

I was angry, and I was angry at God. I saw through the stories and dogma that they had taught me as truth. I was angry because the adults not only failed to keep me safe, but in the mind of my brain as a child, so did God. How could God allow this man to represent him, to stand in the house of God, and do the awful things he did? I decided that day that I was done with the church. I was done with Christianity.

RELIGIOUS DOGMA, SOCIAL NORMS, & FEAR...OH MY!

Quitting Christianity is like quitting any other cult. For many reading this, you know how much it stung. It's true of many other religions. The reason that it stings for some is that religion is built on dogma.

Dogmas are belief structures with key characteristics. Some of those characteristics include that the belief structure is absolute truth, absolutely essential, and that you cannot question. Should you ever dare to question or challenge them, there is some horrible consequence that awaits you. (Sound familiar? Like eternal damnation?)

Dogmas and belief structures are connected to social norms. Just like we were taught that it's only safe if we follow the rules in society, as I discussed earlier, we're also taught that there is safety and comfort in believing the beliefs of the culture we are raised in. We are taught to believe beliefs of not only the culture and society, but also of the subcultures, religions, and even countercultures. (An example of a counterculture would be the Amish, who have their own set of social norms, culture, and religion that is counter, or opposing, to that of mainstream culture.)

This process, of being taught to believe the norms, values, and beliefs of cultures and groups that we belong to, is called socialization.

The adults are not trying to hurt us by teaching us to be "good humans" and follow society's rules. They are also not trying to hurt us by teaching us to believe certain things. In fact, it's quite the opposite. Generation after generation after generation has learned, often painfully, that this is how you stay safe.

For example, it made sense to teach the next generation that when fire burns you, it hurts. Or that stealing things is wrong (because it prevents stealing) or that murder is wrong (because it prevents murder). We didn't stop there as humans. We passed down all of the social rules and beliefs that our brains told us kept us safe—generation after generation—even when those things were actually causing harm.

Racism is a great example of this. People who believe in racist ideology fall on a spectrum.

Some people fully understand that they believe in racial superiority, and they believe this is a requirement in order for their children to have the best life. Therefore they pass this belief to their children while others call that same belief hate.

Parents, like my mom, taught me the opposite belief. She believed in order for us to have the best life, we needed to believe in love and inclusion.

There are many people who are somewhere between the two. They had parents, grandparents, and great-grandparents who had been passing down beliefs about race for generations. As society changed, so too did the way they taught those beliefs and what was taught about them—because they wanted to keep the people they loved safe.

People need to share their beliefs, but also balance them with how to believe them in society.

And religious beliefs and dogma are not exempt from the things that get passed down generationally. The challenge comes when our families or society get it wrong. Let's look at slavery using the racism example above. The United States (among other places) is still trying to undo all the social programming and generational sharing of beliefs that supported a social structure that justified slavery. Just because we decided it was no longer legal didn't instantaneously change the belief structures of millions of people.

We find this with the beliefs tied up in spirituality, too. I went to school with friends who were not allowed to play cards, dance, or even sing because their families considered it sinful. And they had been taught that from their parents, who learned it from their parents, and so on and so forth. And I went to school with others who could do all of those things and whose parents thought the other kids' parents were wrong and mistaken. Both groups were based on belief systems and unexamined dogma.

The real trouble is no one was willing to say, "You can choose that!" or "This is just what we believe." (Because with Dogma and Religion, remember, the belief is unquestionable.)

Thoughts like this create fear because there are a lot of unanswered questions that society hasn't equipped people (or religion) to answer.

Many people become very uncomfortable when they realize this and have to face the social contrast when it surfaces. It's challenging when some family members believe one thing and behave a certain way, while others believe and behave in a contradictory way. It's a lot easier if everyone is "the same."

It's back to sameness and the false comfort it provides that humankind gravitates to.

We don't have to repeat this, though.

When we face the discomfort that we sometimes feel when we notice our differences, we can build tolerance and skills to strengthen ourselves. I teach people HOW to notice that pattern in our thinking and to investigate it. When we realize we aren't the same at all, it creates a normalcy in the differences between us, and there is a beautiful value in owning that. It reduces fear and anxiety and also creates a more tolerant social group and society where it's okay to believe different things.

Quitting Christianity

When I left the church and Christianity, it was a conscious decision I made at nine years old. It was a bit like breaking up with your toxic ex, and I even tried to go back more than once. When I was in high school, I went to church with various friends and tried out their churches.

No one was talking about religious trauma back then, which is what happens when the religious leader is the abuser.

What no one told me is that when you experience this, you can't just pretend you're okay. You can't go back to church and think it's going to not be traumatic. Each time, it was more awful than the time before and I just ended up angrier, because I wasn't actually dealing with the religious trauma.

Everyone around me was helping me deal with the other traumas, but no one thought about helping a child deal with religious trauma. Honestly, I don't know if anyone in the '90s even understood the concept.

Thankfully, I figured out that it was a bad idea, and I took a good long time away. The only time I went back was a few times with a guy I dated in college because his mom was insistent that I go to mass with them.

I continued to avoid church until I finally found a healing church in graduate school.

HEALING BEYOND DOGMA

What made the church experience in grad school different? It was absent of dogma. This church was founded on principles like social justice, collective consciousness, unity, diversity, compassion, and love. They taught about a wide variety of world religions (even paganism). And they did it in order to provide people with a thorough foundation and show the similarities between them.

That is where the real moment of spiritual awakening clicked for me. That was the moment I looked at my partner at the time and said, "Holy fuck, they are just different paths that are all leading people home. To the same home."

I still get teary and choked up, thinking back to that moment. It's one of the most spiritual moments I've had, sitting on the pew in that sanctuary, with the sun shining in the stained glass windows. I remember thinking *if only I could tell the world that we don't have to fight. We're on the same team. We are just speaking a different language because our grandparents had different versions of stories they told us to teach us similar lessons.*

I could choose to be angry and bitter. I have every reason based on the way my grandfather, who was my minister, ripped away my childhood innocence, stole decades of my spiritual connection from me, and nearly stole a calling of spiritual leadership. (Some things are greater than man.) And yet, I chose to let it go.

Over the years, I chose to do the work and heal the layers of trauma, including the spiritual trauma, in me. And in doing so, I now can say "God." It was a word that, for the better part of a decade and a half, triggered me so badly that I couldn't say it, and I asked those around me not to say it, either. Not only can I now say "God," but I can MEAN God. When I say it, there is no charge. I mean God, Source, Allah, Goddess, Universe, All That Is, a Higher Power, the Oneness in each of us that connects us to each other and to everything else.

Beyond that, however, I understand with blinding clarity the path religion and dogma are on. I understand deep within my bones and spirit that it is causing both individual and collective traumas similar to the one I experienced. It is the trauma billions of humans have experienced over thousands of years in the name of religion and religious wars— official and unofficial. And I understand the truth that all the paths are leading us home. Yes, the stories may vary. But in the end, we're all going to the same place, and we're all walking the same path home.

We know what the future looks like if we continue this path of dogma dog versus dogma dog. Where your "dogma dog" is in a dogfight with my "dogma dog," and we are the casualties of this dog-fighting spiritual war. We know because we've seen it play out in history for thousands of years. We know because we watch it play out in the news, and on social media, every single day around the world.

Religion is used to justify genocides, mass shootings, honor killings, terrorism, and so much more. We know what this looks like because it's been used to justify the crusades and "missions." And the atrocities by our "leaders" taking indigenous children from their families to place them in schools around the world, including Canada and the U.S. We know what the future looks like with religious dogma running the show.

What if we quit religious dogma? Instead, what if we shifted toward a spiritual approach free of dogma? My vision looks like people being empowered and taught how to choose their own principles, morals, and values. And people learning about the world cultures and traditions—with no one being better than any other. What if we taught people there were many paths to get home when they were finished here on earth, and all paths were equally valid, and they got to choose which path they could walk home? And how beautiful would it be if we could walk beside one another, each on our own path, in peace?

This would almost certainly not be easy. Religious leaders have power, and no one with power wants to give that up. Additionally, religions are also financial institutions. They've woven themselves and their dogmas deeply into the fabric of societies around the world. It's taken thousands of years to stand these dogmas up, and I do not expect that we would dismantle them quickly.

This is the work of the future.

The work is to move beyond the wounded, traumatized world where people are fighting over their dogma being better than someone else's dogma. This is the work to move beyond people being traumatized by the individual pain that the dogmas are causing. This is the work to allow a more organic, spiritually healed future for humanity.

Let us create a world where we encourage gifted children to be gifted and adults to own their spiritual gifts. Where healers walk among doctors, and shamans among psychologists. Let us all learn to own a more complete version of our whole authentic selves.

This is the world I dream of for our future and for our children's futures. A world where our children never have to feel different or feel shame because they don't "fit in." A world where parents all have the knowledge about spiritual gifts and spirituality or have access to resources that other people have. This is our future if we are willing to do the work to create it.

THIS IS WHAT LIES BEYOND

Exercise to explore what lies beyond:

In order to explore what lies beyond, we must first ask what lies within and excavate that. We must be willing to look honestly at what is within us, why it is there, and where it came from. From there, we must ask if we want to keep it and if it makes sense for us to keep it. It often helps to ask what function it's serving currently and what function it has served in the past. This is one of the processes that I teach inside of my signature program, Vision. And as I explain to the participants in that program, it is a lifelong process.

When I was writing the chapter for this book, I wanted to give you a taste of what that is like. And so, I am including the following questions for you to reflect upon and journal about.

BEYOND THE SHIFT

The secret to this exercise is to approach it with the curiosity of a toddler. That means to ask why, a lot! "Why? But why? Why is that? How come? But why? Why? Why? Well, why is that?"

If you've ever been with a toddler or even a young child, you know what I am referring to. If not, just keep going deeper down the rabbit hole!

Questions to ask yourself:

1. Do humans have souls? How do you know? Where did you learn that?

2. What have you learned about souls over the course of your life?

3. Who taught you about souls? Have different people taught you different things?

4. Has your understanding of souls changed over time?

5. If humans do not have souls, what makes them "human"?

6. If humans do not have souls, do you believe they have some kind of essence that makes them different than a rock?

7. If humans do have souls, do you think rocks do or do not have souls?

8. How do you know these things?

9. Do all or no humans have souls?

10. Can a human lose their soul? If a human started with a soul and lost a soul, are they still human?

11. Do you talk to your friends and family about these topics? Why or why not? Do you all have a similar perspective? How are they similar or different? Why do you believe that is?

After you've journaled on your answers, use these questions to reflect on your responses to discover what you learned about yourself.

◊ What did you learn?

◊ Did you see any signs of dogma or dogma that you'd been exposed to in your past at any point?

◊ Did you find yourself thinking about how different people might have different beliefs about souls or even the origin of human beings?

◊ Is it possible that two people could believe different things about this topic and still have much to learn from one another, be friends, or find commonalities?

◊ Is it possible that your answers and beliefs could be true for you, and theirs true for them, and neither be more true than the other?

◊ If you believe that your truth is the truth and that you can be tolerant of others but that yours is the correct truth, it's a sign you may need to ask yourself if there are elements of dogma at play. And if there are, if you want to accept that, or not. It's a choice. You get to decide. Do you want to go beyond the dogma?

ABOUT ANGELA KAYE SIMON
B.A., B.S., M.A., G.C., PhD(C-ABD)

Angela's career began as an academic. In the early part of her career, she taught sociology, gender & women's studies, and interdisciplinary courses at multiple universities and colleges in the United States. As an academic, Angela's role as a truth-teller and spiritual leader had already begun to shine through. She challenged tradition as she pushed for interdisciplinary programs and courses, and she challenged institutional systems of oppression within academia.

After an accident in 2009, Angela left academia to recover from a traumatic brain injury. It was that experience that allowed her to ask deep questions and step into a different path of coaching. Her favorite part of her time at the university was the impact she made on her students, and she discovered through coaching she could have that same impact and be considerably more happy.

Angela now runs multiple businesses as an international spiritual leader. She has combined her expertise as a sociologist, with her lifelong gifts as a powerful psychic medium, to create something truly magickal.

ABOUT ANGELA KAYE SIMON

Angela is revolutionizing the world (and universe) one person and soul at a time. By teaching people how to identify, excavate, and intentionally shift their programming, she provides both a theoretical framework and actionable tools that allow people to shift beyond the limitations of the 3D world. As a quantum-informed practitioner, she also believes in educating and empowering people to understand from the start that the 5D is NOT a destination and that there is so much more to expand beyond in our universe, and our lifetimes. Through this work, she empowers people to revolutionize their lives, relationships, spirituality, magick, and even their businesses.

Angela understands that in order to support herself in this mission, self care is essential. When she's not working she can be found enjoying her furry friends, building out her eco-homestead, cooking, gardening, volunteering, and finding other innovative ways to impact the world!

You can learn more about Angela on her various social media channels and her website:

www.TheIntuitiveCreatrix.com

THE INTUITIVE BEYOND

MAGICKAL CRYSTAL HEALING
BY KARINA GARCÍA DEL PEZO, ACM

I was driving through my hometown for no reason other than needing to get out of my head. I was on Main Street sitting at a stoplight when suddenly, I heard a loud voice in my head say, "Turn left."

It scared me, and I remember turning around as if I was looking for a person in my backseat! I heard the voice again, so I did what any rational person would do and turned left. I heard a series of directions and wound up at a small, empty store. There was a large sign that read "for rent." Chills ran through my body as I heard the word "Incantations." Filled with excitement, I wrote down the number and headed back home.

It was the turning point that led me to you.

My name is Karina Guadalupe Garcia Del Pezo. Yes, that is a mouthful, and it took me what feels like a lifetime to understand the power behind my name.

I am a Mexican-American Crystal Shaman—a mother, a wife, and I AM a magickal crystal woman.

Please know that if you are reading this book it is for a good reason. And if you are curious about crystals, you are meant to work with them! I understand your fears and doubts as I have experienced them.

MAGICKAL CRYSTAL HEALING

I come from a family of geologists, but I didn't always appreciate crystals for their healing frequencies. Nor did I understand they would become powerful catalysts for my spiritual journey.

I grew up in Westchester, New York. My family is predominantly Catholic, but I always had a thirst for esoteric knowledge. I knew deep inside that ancient secrets, wisdom, and healing were waiting to be discovered. Life had so much more to offer me than my regular 9-5 and the stagnant life I was currently living.

In my early twenties, I had everything that most people wanted. I married my high school sweetheart, and we had three beautiful children. My career was solid and secure, and people highly respected me. I managed a successful veterinary practice with good pay, medical insurance for my family, and lovely clients. My boss was supportive, and our staff was my extended family.

I was truly blessed, but....

I felt incredibly empty, like I was existing but not living. I wasn't in alignment with my joy, spiritual path, or purpose. That made me feel incredibly alone despite all the love and support surrounding me.

I was an ambitious soul born with an unquenchable thirst for spirit. I could feel the Earth's pulsating heartbeat underneath my bare feet calling me back home.

I could hear ancient songs carried by the wind whispering in my ears. Literally! The sound of tribal drums would awake me in the early hours.

The Earth was alive, communicating, and I yearned to know the truth about myself, my purpose, and how to heal. It felt as if the truth was right there, so close, but I had no way of reaching it.

One of my biggest problems was not knowing myself or trusting my feelings. No one taught any of what I was experiencing, and I didn't know anyone who could relate to what I was experiencing.

For most of my young adult life, I bounced back and forth, joining many religions and spiritual paths, but none satisfied the blaze within my heart. I left like I was spiritually starving.

Crystal Clear Remembering

One day, my son Lucas, who was in first grade, came home from a field trip with an amethyst for me. He had purchased it at the museum gift shop. He made me close my eyes and placed it in my hand. I'll never forget his excitement!

I could feel the amethyst pulsating in my hands. It felt as if I could hear my heartbeat in my ears. My heart was racing, and I didn't understand why.

I now realize this was one of my first awakenings. The amethyst activated frequencies and forgotten memories. My current self was remembering my purpose and sending me what felt like a crystal clear message. Finally!

That was the day I remembered the power of Crystal Healing.

MAGICKAL CRYSTAL HEALING

My crystal journey began when I started collecting crystals and rocks. Working with each crystal individually taught me that each had its own personality, vibe, and message. I read all the crystal information available to me and took many classes. What blew my mind the most was that what I was experiencing with crystals on my own was very similar to what was written in books and the classes I took. If most people were experiencing the same, then it had to be true! I wasn't alone.

Little by little, I started making changes in my life based on their guidance and began to feel better physically. I learned more about myself intimately and finally felt spiritually full and vibrant. I found my passion!

However, my circle of friends was getting smaller. My relationship with my husband was rockier than ever. It was as if I were slowly shedding old ways of being on every level. The relationships and activities that once satisfied me no longer resonated with the person I was becoming. That was hard to understand at the time. In my mind, I expected "healing" to feel like cupcakes and unicorns.

I was definitely out of my comfort zone and feeling very uncertain about where all of this was heading. The one thing I knew with certainty was that I started loving this new version of myself, and I would not give her up!

So, I dug even deeper. I asked my spirit guides for support with all my relationships and abundance in all areas of my life that were for my highest path.

I went back to my Afro-Mexican roots and fell in love with working with healing herbs, oils, and candles. As I was learning more about energy healing techniques and the abundance of the universe, I understood our limitless capabilities. I became a certified Crystal Healer, Reiki Master, Akashic Records Practitioner, and tarot reader. My online audience grew as I spoke to whoever would listen to my passion and watch my live videos on social media platforms. I did all this despite my fear of appearing on camera and public speaking. I joined like-minded groups for support, and eventually, I created my own healing groups and welcomed all!

I dreamed of a physical crystal healing practice and wanted to be of service. I yearned to share my healing and passion for crystals with my community. But, could I quit my secure job? How could I afford healthcare for my family? What if my marriage fell apart because I was so different? Could I afford another rent? I didn't even know where or how to buy crystals in bulk. Who would take me seriously? What if no one signed up for my healing services? What if I failed?

As much as I loved the veterinary practice and everyone in it, I knew I could no longer play that role. Despite my biggest fears, I resigned.

This scared me out of my mind! I had no idea where I was going to come up with money or how I was going to attract clients, but I clung on to my faith like my life depended on it.

I quit the same day I went for that drive and heard the voice urging me to "turn left." I called the number right away, and I explained what my intentions were for the space my intuition had led me to. The owner of the establishment was kind, and the rent was surprisingly within my budget. We signed a contract, and I had keys to my crystal sanctuary within a week!

I asked my spirit guides for the meaning of the word "incantations." I heard "the magickal words spoken. Use your words and energy to create your most magnificent life."

And so, of course, I named the store "Incantations."

As if that wasn't miraculous enough, within a few days, I received a large check from one of the most generous people I've ever met in my life. I would soon know her as my Earth angel. She believed in me and what I offered!

With that check, I was able to buy inventory and upgrade my crystal shop.

Open For Business

My soul clients did show up! Most purchased healing packages of four to eight sessions, and everyone purchased crystals with every visit! I held workshops and private sessions. I soon started teaching online courses and teaching my clients.

Fast forwarding five years, I am beyond grateful that I took the leap! I now work from home as a full-time energy healer and teacher. I have evolved tremendously in my own spiritual practice. Along the way, I learned numerology and am currently immersed in astrology. I love combining crystals with all the modalities I have learned. My company's name has changed and is now Terra Nova Crystals.

BEYOND THE SHIFT

I decided to change the name of my company to Terra Nova Crystals because my spiritual journey has evolved and although Incantations will forever be ingrained in my heart, I can feel a change in the collective's energy, too. I believe this shift is part of a new golden age we are entering. The word Terra means earth or land, and Nova is a transient astronomical event that causes the sudden appearance of a bright, "new" star. (Hence the name "nova," which is Latin for "new.")

My crystals are birthed from Earth but my teachings, spirituality, and healing techniques are a combination of Spirit, galactic healing, and Earth magick. I want my business to reflect these concepts.

My personal relationships with crystal miners are now worldwide. These connections allow me to provide the most gorgeous soul crystals for my clients and their practices. I have had the tremendous honor of holding space for hundreds of clients and students and I feel incredibly satisfied.

My family is whole. My children are my joy, and my marriage has never been more loving.

The journey to get here was NOT easy, and it didn't happen overnight. I fell on my butt many times, but each time got up a little more gracefully. I had to learn to surrender my fears and trust in the divine. There were many tears shed, arguments, and a ton of self-doubt, but it was all worth it. The hardest lessons were my most valuable teachers. I am forever grateful to the mineral kingdom.

WHAT IS CRYSTAL HEALING AND HOW DOES IT WORK?

Crystal healing is a holistic and natural therapy that involves using various types of crystals, gemstones, minerals, or rocks to promote physical, emotional, and spiritual well-being.

It has ancient roots leading back to Egypt and the times of Lemuria. It is based on the belief that crystals possess frequencies or energies that affect a person's chakras and energy field. There are zero side effects with this form of holistic therapy, and it is truly limitless.

Working with crystals can enhance your life to:
- ◊ achieve a harmonious life
- ◊ manifest desired goals
- ◊ create financial prosperity
- ◊ use as protection
- ◊ find love
- ◊ work with the subconscious mind
- ◊ heal emotional blocks
- ◊ build confidence
- ◊ create a transformative spiritual path.

Crystal healing is not intended to replace medical treatment. It is, however, excellent as an additional support for improving holistic well-being.

Crystals help one anchor into oneself for balance and wisdom. They assist one in tuning out the world's external confusion and tuning into one's unique and authentic expression. Crystals are teachers, allies, and keepers of wisdom and time.

How to select a crystal:

Mother Earth is very generous. She has provided us with an abundance of crystals and rocks to heal with. Each crystal has a unique vibration, use, and purpose. We can utilize its vibration to help raise our frequency to match its vibration. This is called crystal entrainment. Our body naturally wants to heal and vibrate at a higher frequency.

This means that by having a crystal on us or within our environment, our bodies will try to naturally attune themselves to that vibration.

I recommend using one crystal at a time for a minimum of twenty-one days.

Questions to journal to help you in selecting your crystal:

1. What is your intention?

2. What are you currently experiencing?

3. What would you like to heal or balance within yourself?

4. How would you like to feel?

5. What would you like to experience?

6. If you are visual, is there a certain color coming through as you answer these questions?

Keep a journal and record thoughts, feelings, visions, and sensations while working with your crystal. You may want to record your sleeping pattern and dreams.

Reflect on your reality.

1. Are there any shifts or changes happening in your life?

2. Are you noticing synchronicities?

3. Are you being triggered?

4. How are you responding?

5. Are you manifesting more quickly?

Recording it in a journal will serve for self-reflection and proof of what does and doesn't work for you.

INTUITION AND CRYSTALS

My favorite way of selecting a crystal is through intuition. Your intellectual mind may not understand why you chose that particular crystal, but it's always right! The more you practice, the more natural and fun it becomes.

1: Set Your Intention:

Before you begin, set a clear intention for why you want a crystal. Are you seeking healing, protection, love, abundance, or any other specific purpose? This intention will guide your intuitive process.

2: Relax and center your energy:

Find a quiet and peaceful space where you can relax. Take three deep breaths in through your nose and out through your mouth to center yourself. This will help you in clearing your mind.

3: Observe your senses:

Approach or look at a display of crystals. This can be in a crystal store or online. Remember that energy is limitless, and you can absolutely feel the crystal's energy. Keep an open heart and pay attention to how you feel when you look at or touch a particular crystal. Your intuition will communicate through subtle feelings, emotions, and sensations. Your body may even respond through smell, taste, or hearing.

- ◊ **Physical Sensations:** As you hold or touch different crystals, notice any physical sensations in your body. Some people experience tingling, warmth, coolness, or a gentle vibration when they connect with a crystal that resonates with them.

- ◊ **Visual Attraction:** Allow your gaze to rest on various crystals and observe which ones draw your attention. It might be a particular color, shape, or pattern that stands out to you.

- ◊ **Energy Sensing:** Gently hover your non-dominant hand over a crystal without touching it. Close your eyes and notice if you feel any energy or sensation emanating from the crystal. Trust the impressions you receive.

◊ **Listen to Your Inner Voice:** Pay attention to any thoughts or phrases that come to mind when you focus on a specific crystal. Your inner voice might offer insights or messages about the crystal's significance for you.

◊ **Trust Your Gut Feeling:** Your initial, instinctive reaction to a crystal is often a good indicator. If a crystal feels right and aligns with your intention, trust your gut feeling. Don't convince yourself!

◊ **Stay Open and Patient:** Sometimes, your intuition might guide you to a crystal you didn't expect. Be open to surprises.

◊ **Confirmation:** If you're unsure, you can use a pendulum or muscle testing to ask yes/no questions about which crystal is best for you.

◊ **Connecting:** Once you've chosen a crystal, cleanse it and spend time bonding with it. Then, research its properties and meanings. This can help deepen your connection and understanding of your choice.

Cleansing and Crystal Care

Crystals are energetic beings that absorb and give off energy. The purpose of clearing a crystal is to reset its energy, especially if it is new to you. You want clear and high vibrating energy when working with all crystals.

Methods of Cleansing Crystals:

Smoke Herb Cleansing

Most people call this "smudging," although that is not the correct term. Smoke cleansing was traditionally used by Native American and indigenous peoples. To do this, you simply pass the crystal through the smoke of a cleansing herb such as White Sage, Rosemary, or Palo Santo. I like to use what is abundant in the land and season.

Visualize the smoke purifying the crystal's energy. Make sure you are in a well-ventilated area. Please use a dish to hold the ash or ember. Always consult with a healthcare practitioner prior to working with herbs, especially if you are pregnant or have allergies.

Running Water

This method is best used with natural running water such as a river, ocean, or rain, but tap water will do. Hold the crystal under gently running cold water for a few minutes.

Visualize the water washing away any stagnant energy.

> **Caution:** Not all crystals are suitable for this method because water can damage some crystals.

Sound

Sound is extremely powerful. You can use a singing bowl, drums, bells, Tingshas clapping, or your own unique voice to cleanse and bless a crystal or a space.

Sunlight

Place the crystal in direct sunlight for a few hours. The crystals will absorb natural clearing and charging energies.

Caution: This method may not be suitable for all crystals as the sun may fade the color of bright crystals.

Other Crystals

Some crystals, like Selenite and Obsidian, have the ability to cleanse other crystals. Place the crystal you want to clear on top of a cleansing crystal overnight.

Visualization and Prayer

Hold the crystal in your hands and visualize it being surrounded by bright white or violet light. You may also request the assistance of a spirit guide to help cleanse the crystal. Imagine this divine light cleansing the crystal's energy and restoring it to its natural vibration.

Moonlight

I don't personally feel the Moon cleanses crystals as most people do. I do, however, feel the Moon "charges" crystals. Charging crystals with the lunar energy is like boosting your cell phone battery. The crystal will charge using the Moon's energy.

You can also charge your crystals with planetary and astrological energy. For example, if I want to charge my crystal with the energies of confidence, passion, and luxury, I may charge it under a new or full Moon in Leo.

Leave the crystal outside under the Moon overnight.

CHAKRAS, AFFIRMATIONS, AND CRYSTALS

Chakra Is a Sanskrit word that means "spinning wheel of light." The chakras are a system of interconnected energy centers located along the central axis of the body.

Chakras regulate the function of physical, emotional, mental, and spiritual parts of our being.

Each chakra governs a different function of the body. Each has its own color, frequency, keynote, and crystal that we can use to heal or balance the body.

When our chakras are in alignment, we function at an optimal level. When they are not in alignment, our body may experience disharmony, and our life may feel unbalanced.

We have many chakras, but in this chapter, I will address the seven main chakras and how we can utilize crystal frequencies to bring about balance.

Affirmation:

An affirmation is a positive statement you intentionally repeat to yourself with the goal of influencing your thoughts, beliefs, behaviors, and reality. They are designed to help you shift your mindset by replacing negative or limiting thoughts with more empowering and optimistic ones. Using crystals with intention and affirmation leads to empowering shifts!

The Seven Main Chakras:

1st Chakra: Root Chakra (Muladhara)

Location: The base of the spine.

It is associated with stability, survival, security, money, a sense of belonging, and grounding.

Color: Red (Select crystals that are within the red, black, or brown color spectrum.)

Element: Earth

Key Note: C

Crystals: Garnet, Red Jasper, Hematite, Black Tourmaline, Smokey Quartz, Onyx

Affirmations for the Root Chakra:

I am safe and fully supported by the universe.

I am at peace and whole.

I am exactly where I need to be.

I have everything I need.

I am abundant and prosperous in all areas of my life.

Money flows to me easily.

I am healthy, wealthy, and in alignment with my highest path.

I am grounded in my truth and stand strong in my authenticity.

I am resilient and rooted in my sovereignty.

2ND CHAKRA: SACRAL CHAKRA (SWADHISTHANA)

Location: The lower abdomen.

The sacral chakra is associated with creativity, sensuality, sexual energy, manifesting, emotions, and relationships.

Color: Orange (Select crystals within the orange or red-orange color spectrum.)

Element: Water

Keynote: D

Crystals: Carnelian, Imperial Topaz, Zircon, Orange Calcite, Garnet, Sunstone, Womb Ball (Botryoidal Chalcedony), Shiva Lingam, Peach Moonstone

Affirmations for the Sacral Chakra:

I am bountiful.

I embrace my creativity and allow for it to flow through me with ease.

I deserve pleasure and fully embrace my sexuality.

I am sexy!

My body is a sacred and divine temple.

I am abundant in all areas of my life.

I manifest with joy.

I am beautiful and powerful.

3rd Chakra: Solar Plexus Chakra (Manipura)

Location: Situated in the upper abdomen.

The solar plexus is associated with personal power, confidence, self-esteem, and leadership. This is our powerhouse!

Color: Yellow (Select crystals within the yellow or gold color spectrum.)

Element: Fire

Keynote: E

Crystals: Citrine, Pyrite, Golden Healer, Bumblebee Jasper, Yellow Aventurine, Tiger's Eye

Affirmations for the Solar Plexus Chakra:

I am powerful and courageous.

I trust my gut instincts and follow my intuition.

I am a magnet for opportunities and success.

I am a powerful creator.

I am a compassionate and empowering leader.

I am a powerful and passionate being who manifests everything I desire into existence!

4TH CHAKRA: HEART CHAKRA (ANAHATA)

Location: The center of the chest.

The heart chakra is associated with love, compassion, trust, relationships, and emotional balancing. This is our inner temple and the infinite part of our being.

Color: Green or Pink (Select crystals within the pink and green color spectrum.)

Element: Air

Keynote: F

Crystals: Rose Quartz, Rhodochrosite, Ruby, Green Aventurine, Malachite, Chrysoprase

Affirmations for the Heart Chakra:

I am loved.

I am open to receiving and giving love.

I radiate love, compassion, and kindness abundantly.

I honor my emotions.

My feelings are valid.

I am a channel for love.

I love and forgive myself and others.

I surrender to love and allow the walls around my heart to melt away. I trust in unconditional love.

I am whole.

5th Chakra: Throat Chakra (Vishuddha)

Location: At the throat.

The throat chakra is associated with communication, listening, self-expression, truth, authenticity, and manifesting. The throat chakra is also referred to as the portal of the gods. It is through this chakra that we speak our reality into existence.

Color: Turquoise (Select crystals within the turquoise/light blue color spectrum.)

Element: Ether

Keynote: G

Crystals: Amazonite, Turquoise, Blue Lace Agate, Angelite, Aquamarine, Sodalite

Affirmations for the Throat Chakra:

I speak my reality into existence.

My voice is powerful and beautiful.

I express myself clearly and with confidence.

I communicate my needs and boundaries with confidence.

I listen to others with compassion.

My words inspire and heal others.

6TH CHAKRA: THIRD EYE CHAKRA (AJNA)

Location: Between the eyebrows.

The third eye chakra is associated with intuition, insight, spiritual awareness, illumination, and logic.

Color: Indigo (Select crystals within the indigo color spectrum.)

Element: light or "Avyakata"

Keynote: A

Crystals: Azurite, Sapphire, Lapis Lazuli, Labradorite, Moonstone, Tanzanite

Affirmations for the Third Eye Chakra:

I trust my intuition.

I see beyond all illusion and trust my intuition.

I am in alignment with my soul's purpose and follow my soul's calling.

I see my inner vision and honor my path.

I am a seeker of truth and I am guided to higher knowledge.

I activate my third eye and access higher wisdom.

7th Chakra: Crown Chakra (Sahasrara)

Location: The top of the head.

The crown chakra is related to spiritual connection, consciousness, Spirit, God, and higher states of awareness.

Color: Violet (Select crystals within violet, clear, or white color spectrum.)

Element: No element or thought

Keynote: B

Crystals: Amethyst, Purple Fluorite, Delenite, Clear Quartz, Lemurian Seed, Elestial Quartz, Herkimer Diamond, Scolecite, Moldavite

Affirmations for the Crown Chakra:

I am one with the divine (God/dess, spirit...).

I am in alignment with my higher purpose and trust in the divine (God/dess, Source, Great Spirit...).

I am a co-creator with the universe. I manifest my desires with ease.

I am a divine channel for spirit.

I am a sacred vessel of universal consciousness and divine white light.

HOW TO USE YOUR CRYSTAL WITH CHAKRA BALANCING:

1. Set your intention.

2. Select the first crystal.

3. Select one affirmation.

4. Clear your crystal.

5. Set a timer for ten to twenty minutes. Increase the time as desired.

6. Place the crystal on the body, chakra, or simply hold it.

7. Center your energy while taking a few centering breaths.

8. Once you feel centered, state your affirmation as many times as you feel called. I like to visualize myself experiencing my desired outcome and my body taking in the color or frequency of the crystal.

9. Stay within this energy for ten to twenty minutes or your desired time.

10. When you feel you are complete, please journal.

11. Thank your crystal and yourself!

Note: If you fall asleep during your crystal healing time, that is perfectly fine! Honor your body with rest. Often, your crystal guide or spirit team may want to work with you on a deeper level that requires rest.

Other ways to work with crystals:

◊ Meditation.

◊ Full body crystal body layout.

◊ Full body chakra alignment.

◊ Carrying them in your pocket.

◊ Wearing them in the form of jewelry.

◊ Crystal and herb healing baggies.

◊ Crystal grid.

◊ Distance healing for others, including pets.

◊ Space gridding for abundance and protection.

◊ Sleeping with them near you for a better quality of sleep and healing.

> **Note:** Some crystals may produce lucid dreaming, astral travel, or simply keep you up at night because of their intense energy. For the bedroom, select crystals with a gentle vibration and color.

KARINA'S CRYSTAL DOOR TRIFECTA

I downloaded this technique as I started seeing clients on a more regular basis. I needed something to clear my space and also my clients before they entered my space.

This works on all entrances of a home, particular rooms, or work space.

What you will need:

◊   One small flat Selenite stick.

◊   Two pieces of your favorite protective and grounding crystal (Black Tourmaline, Smoky Quartz, Black Obsidian).

◊   A natural Clear Quartz point.

Intention: To create a grounding, energetic filter and protective barrier for myself, my space, and clients prior to them stepping into my sacred space.

1.   Cleanse your crystals and the entrance.

2.   Center your energy.

3.   Hold the crystals in your hand and share with them what you would like them to do.

"Thank you for being on my journey. I give you permission to be the gatekeepers of my space. May all who enter this sacred space experience peace and harmony. May they dissolve all hooks and cords tied to anything less than love. May we all be blessed with an abundance of healing."

4.   Place the Selenite on the top of the door entrance. You may secure it with wall putty or tape.

5.   Place one crystal on the left and right bottom corners of the door.

6.   Hold your Clear Quartz in your dominant hand and activate your crystal door trifecta.

7. Imagine that a beam of powerful light is radiating from the Clear Quartz point.

8. Point your clear Quartz point starting at the bottom left crystal and draw the energy up until you energetically connect to the Selenite. (Your Clear Quartz point does not have to touch the crystals.)

9. Come back to the bottom left and connect the line to the bottom right crystal and then up to the selenite.

You have energetically created a triangle. The triangle or pyramid is a protective and powerful sacred geometric shape.

You may change the bottom crystals to fit your needs.

I recommend you reactivate the crystal trifecta every full Moon, or at the minimum, with every turn of the season.

You may also do the same for creating a prosperity or love door crystal trifecta.

Simply select prosperity or love crystals to attract those frequencies to you and your space.

CRYSTALS THAT ARE ABUNDANT AND ACCESSIBLE TO MOST PEOPLE WORLDWIDE.

Crystals For Love:

Rose Quartz: Love, friendship, inner child healing, emotional balancing, eases worry.

Ruby: Ancestral healing, finding your passion, refilling your love energy.

Green Aventurine: Helps all things grow, including love, prosperity, and even plants.

Ruby Fuschite: Heart chakra activator that supports one in releasing old patterns, fears, programming, and codependency. Love, passion, self-acceptance, ancestral guidance, confidence, self-value.

Crystals For Prosperity:

Citrine: Known as the merchant's stone, natural Citrine is prized for its luxurious wealth-attracting energy. Confidence, creativity, leadership, financial prosperity.

Pyrite: Good fortune, confidence, vitality, grounding, creating ideas.

Prehnite with Epidote: Manifests more of what you already have. Financial prosperity. Helps one in identifying limiting beliefs.

Golden Apatite: Manifesting joy, creativity, financial prosperity.

Crystals For Protection:

Smoky Quartz: Grounding, filters energy, psychic protection, guardian.

Black Tourmaline: Psychic protection, grounding, helps one feel safe.

Jet: Cloaks energy, energy filter, lighter in weight than other protection crystals.

Black Obsidian: Protection, grounding, ancestral healing and guidance, divination.

Amethyst: Psychic protection, helps one in releasing toxic patterns and limiting beliefs.

Crystals For Developing Your Spiritual Senses:

Amethyst: Clears and activates the third eye and crown chakra.

Labradorite: Helps one see through illusion, helps one to develop all psychic senses, shadow work, astral travel, protection.

Elestial Quartz: Can activate remembrance from past lives, integrating gifts and soul lessons, may activate dormant spiritual DNA, may help channel healing frequencies from higher realms or beings.

Clear Quartz: Can be used on all chakras, raises vibration, can mimic all crystals, easily programmable.

FINAL THOUGHTS TO INSPIRE YOU

There are many ways to incorporate and enhance your life with the use of crystals.

There are many ways of healing. Choose what feels right for YOU.

You are limitless, and all things are possible.

Your ideas, dreams, and passions are divinely inspired and supported.

Do more of the things that light you up.

Do things that bring the best out of you.

Do the things that make your heart beat out of your chest with joy and excitement!

Do the things that make you "weird" because those things are your gift and contribution to our planet.

Step into YOUR truth and your unlimited potential. Trust in your heart. The answers are there waiting for you. Live your most magnificent journey.

I wish all of this and greater for you.

Karina G Del Pezo, ACM

ABOUT KARINA G DEL PEZO, ACM

As the Founder of Terra Nova Crystals, an online crystal shop, Karina helps people connect to their soul crystals through live sales and private consultations. She teaches online spiritual courses and workshops, and also provides Shamanic Crystal Reiki healing sessions.

Karina is a multi-accredited Advanced Crystal Master, Crystal Shaman, Reiki Master, Akashic Records Practitioner, Crystal Sound Healer, Tarot Advisor, and Numerologist. She weaves these modalities together to create unique healing experiences for her clients.

What she enjoys most about her journey is witnessing her clients as they discover their spiritual path and empowerment through vibrational healing.

Outside of her professional pursuits, she finds joy and serenity in the calming embrace of nature. She has a deep appreciation for the ocean, animals, and working with her garden.

Karina's contribution in this lifetime is self discovery through crystals and Earth's Healing Magick.

Karina Garcia Del Pezo, ACM
Website: https://terranovacrystals.rocks/
Social Media: https://linktr.ee/incantations.co

BREAKING THE CHAINS
A Journey of Healing and Liberation
by Ingrid Toledo-Hammett

~ So here you are. You say you aren't afraid. Spirituality revealed that man, the one who hurt you. You were so little! You say you aren't afraid to perish or repercussions, so write. Pour it out. Let it break your bones like that demon in your stories. That demon is still creating havoc in your mind and body. In your brain.

Your heart is broken, and not this man, nor another hundred will fix that because it isn't love you lack. It is courage. It is truth, autonomy, authenticity. Stop pretending to be. Just be!

It's exhausting! Aren't you tired? We're tired for you! How long? Do you not understand? They do not want you to speak your truth. They just tried to silence you again. They won't stop. You must stop. Why do you feel the need to protect and apologize? For what, for who? They lied to you. The life you believed to be true, the promises, they weren't real. That life didn't exist. You were thrown amongst the wolves, not sheep. Stop. They weren't good people. You were the good among them. This is all a dream you will soon wake up from, but first, you must write this chapter.

You have truth to speak, so Speak it! Evil to reveal, Reveal it! Write your masterpiece. Let go of the outcome. Surrender.

BREAKING THE CHAINS

Dear Reader,

I am Ingrid, the author of this chapter. It's an honor to share time and space with you.

Full disclosure; I am so very frustrated right now. I am frustrated at the fact that even as I sit here, beginning to write the most important chapter of my life, I'm not entirely free. I want to write the most authentic chapter so that you, my reader, and all readers aligned with this book, may draw courage from my experience. But how can I be transparent without bringing to light the fact that, at this very moment, I am still struggling with the very thing I'm wanting to release you from? I want to be authentic! Do as I say, and not as I do? Most certainly NOT!

Here lies the ugly truth about indoctrination and its harsh reality. I survived an abusive childhood, sexual abuse by a family member and church elder, a violent marriage, and much loss and hardship. Even after all that, the one and only thing holding me back from standing fully in my power and speaking my truth is In-doc-tri-na-tion!

You may think, *That's a whole lot of living and enduring.*

And it certainly is!

So why can't I shake indoctrination? That's an excellent question! I am asking myself the same question at this very moment!

Indoctrination is so deeply rooted in me that even today, after all the inner work I've done, I feel held back and fearful to speak my truth. Even after this amazing opportunity falls into my lap.

That's why I am conjuring up every single ounce of courage and faith left in me at this very moment.

'I call upon Source, Mother Gaia, my Higher Self, my ancestors, guides, galactic council, ascended masters, mentors, teachers, ancient wise mothers, and spirit animals, I need you ALL right now! I want to set myself and those who resonate free once and for all! This chapter, and also you, my reader, will bear witness!'

I was born on the beautiful Caribbean island of Puerto Rico. This lifetime, I chose to be born to parents who never learned to heal their own inflicted or inherited trauma, and began to heal late in life. A traumatized mother who, at a preteen age found the body of her own father after he had committed suicide. And a deeply wounded father, who is still hurting from mistakes, missed opportunities, and the abuse inflicted on him by his father—my grandfather— whom I adored.

The things we don't know as children are the very things that help us understand our parents and have more empathy later in life.

I was raised in a misogynistic culture, surrounded by many gifted yet colonized native indigenous people back in the '70s. Not old, not yet modern. Puerto Rico has changed very much since then.

My parents came from very modest means, direct descendants of Spaniard colonizers, Arawak natives of the island (also called Tainos), and African slaves brought to the island by colonizers.

BREAKING THE CHAINS

I come from a long line of healers, mediums, leaders, and warriors. And also from a long line of strong, intelligent, willful, courageous people, and more than a few misguided followers.

My parents began to study the bible with Jehovah's Witnesses when I was a toddler. I believe they were baptized under that faith before I was four years old. I remember going out in service door-to-door, attending meetings at the Kingdom Hall (which is what witnesses call their place of worship), and traveling in school buses to Circuit and District conventions.

Those were the very best times of my life for a very long time. It was all I ever wanted to be involved in and with, and I truly enjoyed it all! My desire to be in good standing with our Creator was all that ever mattered to me, even at a very young age. I attribute a lot of the good parts of me—such as discipline, respect, and devotion—to having grown up as a witness.

I got baptized at twelve, and was proud of myself! Only after baptism could I serve in Bethel in Brooklyn, NY, or Pioneer. And maybe even attend Gilead, the missionary school! All great privileges!

Pioneering is when you dedicate your time to door-to-door service, either part-time or full-time. Missionaries traveled the world spreading "the truth", which is what witnesses call their teachings. Bethel was where they printed and distributed most of the literature to all the congregations worldwide.

Serving in Bethel was my ultimate dream. My greatest desire!

Getting married and having children was on my mind as well, but not as much as serving. However, as a female member of the congregation, they often reminded me that I could better serve as a pioneer, or wife to a faithful servant.

From an early age, I often asked questions. I was thirsty for knowledge, especially when it came to prophecies. Instead of encouraging me to do independent research, they encouraged me to be "meek" and "teachable", like Moses.

Teachable or "easily controlled"? (To this very day, those words trigger me.)

Along with asking too many questions, I often called out "bad behavior" among peers and elders, which labeled me problematic.

Dating in that faith is reserved for marriage only. For women, to date more than one man was frowned upon, however, men could date as many as they saw fit. After all, they were the leaders and heads of households. What a privilege it was to catch their eye!!

Dating couples were never to be left alone, and a chaperone had to always accompany them. Many young girls were married to much older men. Older faithful men that held positions in the organization were the best pickings for the most submissive and faithful girls. My chances to score one of them were slim.

My parents had five children. I'm the eldest.

My father was disfellowshipped during my teenage years, which meant he was shunned from the congregation. This meant that, as a family, we were also shunned. Very few members would associate with us, and if they did, they were almost always counseled not to.

My mother wanted very much to divorce and free herself from this marriage; however, the elders continuously counseled against it. They would convince her to stay and "forgive", which she did. Her forgiveness turned into chronic depression and thoughts of suicide. This turned into hyper-vigilance and stress for me. I took on too much, which was age-inappropriate, but I did it. I'd probably do it again to spare my mother any more hardship.

What do Jehovah's Witnesses believe?

Not in the Trinity. The Father is Jehovah, which is God's name translated to English from Hebrew (Yahweh). Jesus is the Son, and then there's the Holy Spirit. Not three in one, but three separate things. They also believe that 144,000 will reign in heaven with Jehovah and Jesus after the war of Armageddon, and the rest of the faithful will either survive Armageddon or be resurrected to live in Paradise. Those are the promises we all lived for.

Women were to be submissive to their husbands, and children to their parents. The husband was to love his wife, as Jesus loved the congregation, which was seldom the case. Being a submissive wife was never the issue for me. The issue was that most husbands, like my own father, were abusive to their wives and families, and led double lives, shepherding the flock in very strict, hypocritical, and inappropriate ways. Men shepherd the flock, never women.

To be fair, just like in other faiths, some endeavored to follow Christ's example, however, they weren't the majority.

They instructed us on which were appropriate movies, books, music, associations, entertainment, food, clothing, adornment, holidays, etc., or not. All doctrine was provided using literature printed and distributed by the organization, and talks. We studied this literature daily!

Consulting a medium is condemned and is considered sinning against the Holy Spirit. I read it in the bible many times. But what happens when you are born a medium, as I was? What happens then?

Well, first of all, you keep it to yourself. You pray and plead to God to please take it away because you don't want to perish in Armageddon. You don't want the birds to feast on your eyes; oh no! When, and if, you do confide in someone because the things you see and hear are basically driving you to madness, then they label you wicked, "not worthy of grace". Young peers went as far as calling me Jezebel in public.

As a young teenager, I attended every meeting, went door-to-door, even when my parents did not, and conducted bible studies with young children. I still went to school and helped my parents maintain the household.

And still, I was treated as *"She is not a good association. Stay away from her!"*

BREAKING THE CHAINS

We were all discouraged from attending college, encouraged to go to trade school, and also to pioneer full time. My dream was to be an engineer or an architect. I wanted to help my parents, to take us out of poverty, so I decided not to go to trade school. I went to a regular high school to attain the credits I needed for college, while pioneering. What a mistake that was! I was labeled rebellious. For wanting better for my family, while still doing all I was supposed to? Yes.

My point isn't to bash. Let me explain the impact this type of conditioning has on your well-being when:

◊ you grow up believing doctrine fed to you day and night by your parents and peers,

◊ you are told that you are second class and subservient to men,

◊ all the literature you read, the music you listen to and clothes you wear are all dictated, distributed, approved or disapproved by the organization,

◊ your standing in the organization is determined by the very people who oppress you,

◊ the same rules don't apply to all,

◊ you don't have the protection of your parents or elders,

◊ families are torn apart by way of shunning,

◊ family holidays are forbidden—further alienating you,

◊ your value is measured by predators and those who turn a blind eye.

I'll tell you!

In my experience, inclusive of many others, you:

◊ cannot think for yourself and question your every thought,

◊ believe in everything you're told and question nothing,

◊ cannot and aren't prepared to function in normal society,

◊ cannot make your own decisions, nor form your own opinions,

◊ have very poor boundaries, or never learn to say no,

◊ look for others' approval, even if they mistreat you, invalidate you, or take your innocence,

◊ have very low self esteem,

◊ feel powerless, wicked, and unworthy of God's love.

I felt all of these, and so much so, that when I married outside of the faith, in one of my many attempts to free myself, and had my first child, I considered leaving my newborn daughter at the doorstep of a Jehovah's Witness couple just so that her life would be spared, because I, her mother, was unworthy. My own newborn child!!

That's how broken you become!

Jehovah's Witnesses, as children, are taught that humanity's salvation is in their hands.

BREAKING THE CHAINS

It's a heavy burden!

One must never "stumble another", nor be a bad example to the world, or their blood would be on one's hands.

To "stumble another" means that your conduct directly or indirectly negatively affects someone else's spiritual journey. It causes them to leave the faith, or commit a sin, which would cause them to perish on judgment day. That would make one "blood guilty", resulting in your death as well. This phrase has tremendous power and exercises control over the congregation. Because of this belief, some members have taken their own lives, or the lives of their own family, while others live chronically depressed or experience estrangement within the family.

Door-to-door service was mandatory, or we'd lose our privileges, which weren't many to begin with. The responsibility to save the masses was ours. We were kept away from "worldly people" when possible, only associating with those in the congregation, which never prepared us for the real world. It left us naked, naïve, and easy to control. The more we suffered at the hands of the world, the more worthy we'd become.

We grew up alienated, guilt-ridden, and terrified, yet I still longed to belong. I wanted to please God from the bottom of my heart. I wanted to serve and still do. My heart has always been pure. I know that now.

Fast forward to my thirties with two teenage children and a couple of failed marriages. There were many moves, jobs, and lots of loss. Many hardships later, we find ourselves in

Texas. My daughter is afflicted with Crohn's disease. We almost lost her to Crohn's a time or two. Those were very difficult times during which I still attended meetings with the witnesses from time to time. I always went back. It was like home, just not a healthy one.

In the search for a better diet and anything else that would alleviate her affliction, my daughter discovered Reiki as a healing modality. She began to study and eventually became a Reiki Master. I understood little about it except that it was really helping her. I joined one of my daughter's healing circles and witnessed her in a new light. She was so strong, and assisted many people. She impressed me very much, and I was so proud of her!

Fast forward to 2015.

My daughter and her then-husband were living with me during marriage #3. He was a strong, intelligent man, and an alcoholic, which reduced his life to just one word. He battled his addiction off and on until it beat him in January 2015. He committed suicide while we were at home. Witnessing something like that rattled us to the core. Losing him in that way was one of the most difficult things we've ever endured. We survived it, but it has been an uphill battle for all.

While deep in grief, I discovered that after one and a half glasses of wine, I could talk to God! I could be honest and ask questions. I battled with Him for so many nights in my room, asking why, not understanding, demanding answers, crying, and pleading. It was very sad, yet it opened the door for me to talk to the Creator, something I hadn't done since

I was very young. I was told that God wouldn't listen to my prayers anymore, because I was wicked, so I'd stopped praying. And there I was, having full conversations with Him. Respectfully, of course, because I needed answers!

My doctor prescribed many medications to manage grief and shock, and the circumstances surrounding my late husband's passing. I was taking antidepressants, sleeping aids, and more, just so I could function. And yes, I was drinking wine so I could sleep, and talk to God, while on them. It was a very dangerous time for me and my state of mind.

One night, I had a very intense dream where a lady named Huasca was looking for me. I didn't know anyone named Huasca, but she was most definitely looking for me. I woke up with her name on my mind and couldn't shake it! When I mentioned it to my daughter and she heard me say the name, her eyes opened wide!

She asked me, "Do you mean Ayahuasca?"

I had no idea. I had never heard that name before, so I researched it. My mind was blown! Ayahuasca is a plant medicine. Mother had come to me in a dream!

I have always seen things others can't and experienced entities and all kinds of things paranormal. I never felt alone, because I was never technically alone. My children have abilities also, especially my daughter, so I had to teach them how to manage and set clear boundaries with spirit.

After losing my late husband, I could still feel spirits— however, they stayed distant in a circle around me, close but not interacting. They were showing respect during my time of grief. I understand that now. But I never felt so lonely!

While researching, I discovered that to participate in an Ayahuasca ceremony I could not be on antidepressants. I attended a retreat where I met a beautiful Shaman who is a DōTERRA rep who told me about essential oils. I stopped taking all medications and detoxed my body from all pharmaceutical prescriptions adhering to a strict regimen of essential oils and supplements. It took approximately six months before I felt like myself again, but I did it!

Reiki came to mind after my detox. I remembered how my daughter had healed herself and others. I began to study Reiki in 2016, and got serious about it in 2018, obtaining my Master's Certificate. While actively practicing Reiki, I experienced joy and purpose and felt closer to our Creator!

I also studied other modalities and religions. I felt very empowered by what I was learning and practicing, and the difference it made in my life and those I assisted. So much so that I decided to open a botanica business.

I unveiled Botanica Agua Viva in 2018. Preparing spiritual tools for those in need fulfills me tremendously. I began to own my abilities and even cleared space for those afflicted with negative energy in their homes.

I was growing stronger!

Even though I was doing so much for many, I was still functioning from a place of anger, neglect, and pain. I was practicing Reiki on others, but I wasn't spending time to heal myself.

I continued on my path assisting others because I didn't want to see anyone in pain or afraid to live in their own home.

My patterns were clear: I always put other people's needs before mine and didn't take care of myself. I found fulfillment in my work and would not stop.

In 2021, I came across a profile on social media. It was a female Shaman. She proclaimed herself to be a "Modern-Day Exorcist". I had to know more. I googled and followed her on social media. She was legit! I read her stories and felt a connection instantly. She spoke my language!

I took courses on conjuring, voodoo, and hoodoo basics to better assist those afflicted with negative attachments or victims of dark magick. I was learning to reverse or undo dark magick work. It was all very fascinating!

I've had experience with dark entities all my life so learning to banish them was my new focus. I had been doing it unofficially without training, and seeing someone outside of Hollywood doing the same was more than amazing! I wanted to know more!

Lo and behold, the Shaman offered a course at a fraction of what a private one-on-one session with her would cost. What?!! I had to learn from her, and immediately put it on a credit card to enroll in her six-week course entitled, HONE, Honing Our Natural Energy. I could not be more excited, especially to learn about exorcisms!!! I wanted to assist many people and this course would take me there!

Class began in November, 2021. To my surprise, HONE had nothing to do with exorcism. Not a thing! HONE was about deep Shadow Work. Something I never knew I needed.

This work transformed me. She is an efficient trauma-releasing expert. None of us were ready for her no-nonsense approach! My trauma was in my face, and I had to face it!

During this time, many things bubbled up. Things buried long ago came to the surface. Things I didn't want to think or talk about, but most definitely needed to address. Memories of betrayal, abuse, pain, loss, and, you guessed it, indoctrination.

Anyone who knew me knew better than to bring up religion, or my relationship with my father. Talking to me about those subjects would bring out a triggered side that was not pretty. Guess what two subjects kept rising to the surface? I had no choice but to address them head-on.

My father never accepted me having mediumship abilities. He says I speak to demons and allow them to manipulate me. I stopped arguing with him about it a long time ago. The church labeled me wicked for it, so here were the two most difficult topics ever, staring me right in the face!

As a young woman, I didn't feel protected by my parents, and especially not our father. He was quite abusive to my mother and us children. Neglectful and dismissive. I do remember some kindnesses when one of us kids was sick.

I also remember our utilities being shut off many times. My mom didn't work. She spent most of her time in bed, deeply depressed. I am happy to say my mother is a happy, much healthier person now.

My dad lives with lots of regrets. I wish he would work on letting go.

One evening during a speech at the Kingdom Hall I heard something very powerful. The elder giving the talk said these words, and I never forgot them, "A woman who grows up with an absent father may find it difficult to relate to God as Father. A father loves and protects. If she never experienced this in the family unit, how could she be expected to perceive love or protection from a God she cannot see or touch?"

I cried for days.

During my HONE course, many issues came to the surface relating to my relationship with my father and the Creator. My relationship with the Creator had been based on all I had learned as a child, as well as the pain, neglect, abuse, and alienation we were subjected to growing up. That was my experience of God, and His mercy.

Mercy?! What mercy? What love? What forgiveness?

After HONE ended, the real work began, and I remained close to my teacher. With her assistance, and a lot of soul-searching, I have liberated myself from a lot of trauma and a lifetime of oppressive indoctrination.

I married a wonderful man in 2020. Surprisingly, he too grew up in the same faith and speaks my language. He is my first healthy relationship. With his selfless, unconditional love and support, I have made tremendous strides towards living a much healthier life! He is on his own healing journey now.

My children, family, and loved ones also support, acknowledge, and respect my path. My hard work has rippled out to those I love, and I'm breaking generational curses and healing ancestral trauma.

I continue to assist many, but I do it from a place of healing and peace, not unresolved anger or sadness. I live a joyous life and function from a place of flow and gratitude. I've never been happier!

So is there life after indoctrination? Abso-frkn-lutely!

Our best life awaits us all!

How did I get here? It is a journey! I am a work in progress!

It's taken a lot of hard work, tears, and determination, uncovering lots of buried trauma and airing out dusty skeletons. Having difficult conversations, and owning a whole lot of "nasty" we much prefer to ignore.

Was it all worth it?

A million times YES!

What should you do if you find yourself still suffering from the aftermath of indoctrination? Here's what worked for me.

- ◇ First, make a conscious decision to heal. We often adopt a victim mentality and wallow there. Be the victor, not the victim. Decide to do the work, no matter how difficult it gets. Be open to different modalities until you find the one that speaks to your soul.

◊ Next, find a mentor or teacher. Someone who has experience releasing trauma, and by trauma I mean generational, ancestral, abuse, neglect, attachments— all of these. Select wisely. There are many snake oil salesmen and saleswomen out there more interested in your wallet than your well-being. Someone who operates from a place of love, not ego. Do not follow blindly. They are human, just like you.

◊ Find your tribe. Let your company be those who have your best interest at heart. People who celebrate your wins and keep you honest, who love and support you through your good and bad days, who do not judge you or anyone else around them. Those with whom your soul feels safe!

◊ Believe in yourself. Have faith in YOU first! We are taught to have faith in God, Jesus, and many more deities and saints, but never to have faith in ourselves. When we truly heal, we begin to see ourselves anew, in a new light. We begin to appreciate ourselves for who and what we truly are. We learn to have faith in ourselves, rather than give away our power or devotion so readily. The very moment I could have faith in myself, was the very moment I could have faith in the Creator for the first time in my entire life!

◊ Dig deep and empty your cup of all the things that do not serve you. Make room for all your blessings and then serve or assist from that place of plenty. Do not let your cup overfill. Take care of yourself first. Love and extend yourself the same grace you extend others!

◊ When doing your shadow work, do not tackle all your issues at once. You will be overwhelmed and will want to stop. Address one issue at a time. Sit with it. Let it speak to you. Let it tell you everything that it needs to tell you. Listen. Do not interrupt your shadow until it is done speaking to you. Thank it. Honor it. Bless it and let it go. Set it, and yourself, free.

In closing, I'll share with you some channeled messages I've received during my healing journey from my ancestors, galactic council, and more. I hope one or more resonates with you.

~ *To you suffering from indoctrination, trauma, neglect, or suffering period, here you will find comfort, kinship, understanding, and a sense of belonging. You are not evil. You were perfectly created by Source from the very milli-second and instant of life. Draw from these words what your soul needs. You are not what they say you were. You are and have always been pure of heart and intention. You are seeing yourself thru their jealous eyes. Do not adopt those words or thoughts. They are not yours.*

~ *Indoctrination, control, neglect, abuse—those are just words that limit in this realm, and are meant to restrict and control. They are but words. Follow your path to attain a better understanding. To be born again, because die we must many times over, in order to emerge and ascend. Only then may we truly fulfill our divine purpose. Draw from these words the underlying gift. Surrender. Do not be afraid.*

~ Were you labeled a rebel, a freethinker? Did you try your very best yet somehow always fell short of their grace? Did your desire to help others remain intact? There is so much beauty and uniqueness in you. You are light itself, and it hurts their eyes, burns their skin, and reveals their true nature. They fear your transparency, your truth, because all is revealed in the light.

~ Who is stopping you, or are you simply afraid, or inhibited? Be brave, write words of freedom, of courage. Why wouldn't your readers believe you? Why would they doubt you? They too are searching for truth. Those aligned will relate. Why do you procrastinate? Isn't this the opportunity you've always wanted?

~ Remember 1996, in that bottom bedroom office in NJ? You would get up after midnight to write because the kids were asleep, and the house was quiet. You felt at peace. Pages flowed with stories and music lyrics. You still feel those moments when you hear those lyrics. All you wanted was to tell your story. Well, here you are! Write your story! Set yourself free. Take this opportunity, jump, grab it! Stop apologizing for their errors. **It's not about sparing feelings. It's about saving lives!**

Thank you all for being part of my journey and bearing witness to my liberation. End the cycle of indoctrination! Challenge the process! No more Indoctrination!!

Blessed be!
Ingrid

ABOUT INGRID TOLEDO-HAMMETT, AUTHOR

I am passionate about assisting those who suffer from indoctrination, complex trauma, or other forms of attachment.

As a Reiki Master Teacher, I offer both live and pre-recorded courses in English and Spanish. I began my Reiki studies in 2015, received my Master certification in 2018, and will soon be a certified hypnotist under Cal Banyan.

My online botanica store offers an array of spiritual tools to serve in your spiritual practice or journey.

My sole purpose is to assist anyone who is ready to be untangled from indoctrination, or navigate unresolved trauma. I bring in my own brand of magick and spiritual tools using mediumship, remote viewing, and meditation.

I am Agua Viva; Ingrid Witch One!

ABOUT INGRID TOLEDO-HAMMETT, AUTHOR

Contact Information:

Website: www.botanica-aguaviva.com

Email: info@botanica-agua-viva.com

Facebook: https://www.facebook.com/BotanicaAguaViva/

Tiktok: @botanica_agua_viva

IG: @BOTANICAAGUAVIVA

THE FIRST CUTS ARE THE HARDEST
Gaining Clarity While Living Through Loss by Lucie Miłosz Haskins

It was the middle of the 2020 COVID lockdowns and the man who'd captured my 17-year-old heart and had been by my side for over 50 years was gone.

There was no reprieve like we'd had in 2006 when Dean had fallen from high up an extension ladder and hit the back of his head on the flagstone in our backyard. The coup-contra-coup effects had sloshed his brain against his skull repeatedly, severely damaged his brain, and left him in a deep coma for over a month.

Dean had survived that accident, though my Dean never came back fully, and our shared dreams and visions of an easy retirement had evaporated in an instant. Life eventually rearranged itself into a new "normal." I continued to work at home as a freelance book indexer while I settled into the new role of a 24/7 caregiver.

After Dean's unexpected death fourteen years later, I was grateful for the isolation the pandemic provided because I didn't want help or consolation. I just wanted to be left alone to grieve Dean's death in my own way and at my own pace. *To just be.*

If I'd had to deal with others' good intentions in visiting and comforting me during my early grieving, that wouldn't have helped me. As the consummate hostess, I would have shifted my focus outward and tended to each visitor, welcoming them with food and drink. And all those social interactions would have drained me significantly when I was focusing on their needs and not mine.

It took me a year before I was ready to re-enter the world of the living. I knew I needed to start looking forward. To stop looking in that rearview mirror as I contemplated my future. How was I to proceed without Dean—and not waste what remained of my life pining for him? Who was I if I wasn't caring for someone else? Could I fill in that hollow shell I'd become and carve out a life for myself?

PLANNING AND PREPARATION

Rediscovering my bliss

Before anything else, I wanted to do something special for our two kids, their spouses, and our grandchild, who'd also been grieving deeply. The COVID lockdowns had been especially onerous for them, as they would have welcomed the personal support and visits from their numerous friends. I wanted to shift our focus from our loss to something that would remind us of Dean in a loving and comforting way. To honor his life and his impact on all of us.

An idea soon popped into my head.

I could craft memory quilts made from Dean's flannel shirts for all six of us!

After his brain injury, he'd refused to wear any other shirt, even on our hottest days. For fourteen years, everyone had associated Dean with his flannel shirts. By using them, Dean would still be with us, his love imbued in every thread of the fabric. The shirts, transformed into lap quilts, would provide lasting memories and comfort.

I became a woman with a purpose. It was sheer joy to feel competent again in what I was doing. After fourteen years of staying barely one step ahead of Dean's medical and mental issues, it was a welcomed relief from the chronic underlying stress of caregiving. I wasn't being challenged by medical professionals or challenging them when I felt they weren't adequately caring for Dean.

All of it delighted and fascinated me. This was my territory, a mixture of logistical issues with creative aspects. It was a smorgasbord of diversity in tasks to engage me throughout the entire process.

I slipped easily into decisions and organized my project timeline—and no one second-guessed or confronted me.

Doing something I loved created such peace within me.

I started feeling restored and emboldened into making more decisions. I purchased a new sewing machine for the project because, unlike the few quilts I'd sewn and quilted entirely by hand decades ago, I wanted to work faster to complete the quilts more quickly. I didn't feel tied to the quilting process itself. I recognized that I would most enjoy crafting the quilt tops and could hand over the quilting task to my dear friend Mary Ann. She had her own long-arm quilting machine and thrived doing that part of the process.

Making myself and my needs a priority

My first unexpected learning curve came when I had to decide on the space to devote long-term to this sewing project. We'd lived in our three-bedroom home for thirty years. After our kids had grown and moved out, I had claimed the two smaller bedrooms for my home office and craft/meditation room. Dean enjoyed using the large family room for his ham radio and electronic equipment. We all called it the Radio Room.

I initially thought my ideal space might be one of the smaller repurposed bedrooms or the large dining room table, but each proved to be too constrained for the materials and supplies required.

I kept scouting for other locations.

The largest room in the house—Dean's Radio Room—had been unused since his death. It was only after I had investigated all other options and found them unworkable that I considered using it.

I wondered, **Why was I saving this space for him?** Dean was permanently gone. He wasn't coming back. I was still here and could benefit from expanding my quilting project into it. **I realized that even when I was the only player on this stage, I had still cast myself in second place behind my deceased husband.**

What an eye-opening moment that was for me.

This sparked a memory involving a wringer washer we'd purchased when our son Kit was in cloth diapers, and we were stationed in Germany—without easy access to laundry facilities. The wringer washer required I wring out each washed diaper by manually feeding it from the bottom tub to the roller assembly on top.

One day, a large section of my almost waist-length hair accidentally got caught up in the rollers. As the rollers moved relentlessly around, they fed more and more of my hair around them. I couldn't pull my hair out OR find the release lever. I thought the rollers would soon scalp me. I desperately kept hitting wherever and whatever I could reach until, with great relief, I finally hit something that stopped the assembly.

What's ironic about the situation is that I had brought it on myself. *Dean had wanted to buy a modern washer that didn't require manual wringing. But I had insisted the wringer washer was fine because I hadn't wanted to spend all that extra money on myself. I could do it the hard way.*

Even with this recent realization, followed by resolving to put myself first and to start using the Radio Room for my quilting, I didn't immediately clear it out. I started with a small back corner and used his computer desk to place my sewing machine on. I also emptied a few drawers from a nearby desk to stash my quilting supplies.

The first cuts are the hardest—cutting away Dean

The prep work was all done. I had identified everyone's designs and the order to work on them. I naively thought I had completed the hard part.

I knew cutting up his shirts represented a final goodbye to Dean. His shirts were the last tangible cord tying me so strongly to his life force. Once I cut them up, life as I had lived it with Dean would vanish from this earthly plane.

Much to my frustration, **I still wasn't ready to let go.** I stopped dead in my tracks and everything stalled for a few weeks. Obviously, something more was at play, and I spent a lot of time reflecting on why I wasn't letting go. What was I still clinging to that prevented me from proceeding with my project?

Trusting myself above external authority

I thought back to the phone call I'd received on the morning of April 3, 2020. Dean was in a diabetic coma and had been admitted to Trauma-ICU earlier in the week. The hospital had been on total lockdown from the COVID pandemic and didn't allow visitors for any reason. I called in daily for a status update. Dean had been holding his own and had even improved. He'd been transferred to a step-down unit the day before.

The attending physician informed me that Dean's medical condition had taken an unexpected, fatal downturn. Dean was back in Trauma-ICU, and the physician recommended the most humane act would be to withdraw the life-sustaining measures currently in place.

I remembered the eerily similar circumstances with Dean's severe brain injury in 2006. He'd been lying in another Trauma-ICU unit close to death's door that first week.

THE FIRST CUTS ARE THE HARDEST

The neurologists then hadn't held out much hope that he would survive. Or if he did, that he'd probably remain in a vegetative state.

*We'd been married 36 years and had weathered many challenges together. During that horrific week, **I knew I could not allow him to die alone among strangers** and I would be there with him if he were to die. The Trauma-ICU unit had a strict visitation policy with limited hours. Ignoring visitor rules, I remained in his room 24/7 that entire first week—quietly and unobtrusively, sleeping on the floor, and staying out of the way of the medical staff—until the neurologists concluded Dean would survive.*

I recognized the validity of the physician's opinion as Dean lay on his deathbed, and I knew this would be Dean's last day on earth. I had committed myself to being there for Dean all those years ago. I could do no less for him this time around. **I pulled out all the stops** to get permission to enter the hospital at the height of the COVID lockdowns. **I begged his physician to let me be there for Dean and to be able to hold his hand as he passed over. I pleaded. I cried.**

I told the physician our 54-year love story from beginning to end. How we'd met between Dean's tours in Vietnam when I was 17 years old. How I'd been waitressing at a small diner the summer before my senior year in high school, and he had been a seasoned 23-year-old soldier who'd eaten there every day of his two-week training assignment. How, when our eyes first met, I felt as if I'd been struck by a lightning bolt and blushed from head to toe.

I informed the physician how I had stayed with Dean that entire first week after his brain injury, visited him every day for the five additional months he'd remained hospitalized, and cared for him 24/7 in the fourteen years since then.

I held nothing back and was totally vulnerable. My story must have connected with the physician because he found a way to get me approved to enter the hospital premises.

The halls were empty as I made my way to Dean, grateful to be at his bedside. To hold his hand and let both of us feel the warmth of our touch a final time. I murmured endearments and messages of love to him while he remained in a coma and was essentially nonresponsive. The only time I saw any physical response from him was when I told him that he could leave us now. That we loved him so much and were going to miss him, but we were all going to be okay. **We would take care of each other, and he didn't have to worry about us. He could let go.** His closed eyelids blinked a few times, and he was gone shortly afterward. I was there for him as he took his last breath.

I was grateful I had found the courage and stamina to go head-to-head with the hospital authorities this time around. I don't know how others handled being locked out and kept away while their loved ones died alone during the COVID lockdowns. Maybe I would have been the same and acquiesced to authority if my earlier experiences hadn't toughened me. I was SO grateful that I had had those fourteen years to learn how to stand strong and how to be Dean's advocate when he couldn't speak for himself. And to trust that I knew more than any outside authority what Dean needed and how I could help him.

The first cuts are the hardest—cutting away pieces of my hidden/shadow side

After Dean exited his physical form, **I began to guilt myself** for my perceived inadequacies in failing him this final time. **He was gone—and my shameful secret was that it was all my fault. I hadn't found a way to keep him alive.** I lost myself in self-judgment and criticism about how I hadn't deserved him and was now reaping these horrible consequences. Oh, **I'd been there by his side at the end, but when it mattered most, I'd failed him.**

My year of grieving was full of self-recrimination. I had surmounted one crisis after another for fourteen years after his brain injury. But during those last few months, it seemed every effort I made had resulted in yet another door slammed in our faces. If only I'd selected another option or tried harder to find more avenues to explore.

I wanted to disown and remove those hidden, shameful pieces of me. The places I had made the wrong decisions. But, if I pruned them all away, I knew I'd shrink and die because there wouldn't be any *me* left. And I certainly couldn't move forward because I didn't deserve a good life after my failure as a wife and caregiver.

Finally too exhausted to continue berating myself, **I slowly awakened to other perspectives** that had found an opening and trickled in. **Maybe it *wasn't* my fault that Dean had died.** There had been numerous doctors those last few months who'd tended to him—exploring solutions, doing what they could to counteract his downslide. **Maybe all the blame didn't rest on my shoulders.**

One message resonated especially strongly with me. The message was this: **Death is always a personal choice, regardless of how it may appear.**

I thought back to those last tumultuous months leading up to Dean's passing, like a row of dominoes falling slowly and inexorably one into the other. Could Dean, even in his diminished physical state, have orchestrated everything from a soul level? Could he truly have had the choice and influence to do so?

I knew this vital, vibrant man had been tired of living in such a reduced capacity for so many years. **Perhaps Dean hadn't been a victim of circumstances after all but had selected his own exit point.** It made so much sense to me as I absorbed this clarity. Dean wasn't a victim. He was where he wanted to be. While I still deeply grieved his loss, this new possibility also deeply heartened me.

I realized I'd been trying so hard to keep Dean alive that I had missed the possibility that he was ready to leave. That, even in his mentally and physically diminished state, his soul and higher self were there to help him do so. **It had been his life journey and his decision. Not mine.**

I could now forgive myself for clinging so desperately to him those final months, let Dean go completely, and start moving forward with my own journey.

I started cutting up all of Dean's flannel shirts. **The first cuts were definitely the hardest.** But, as I moved through the process, each subsequent cut became easier until I no longer felt sadness or grief when I handled his shirts.

Instead I felt joy that they were no longer languishing in closets and boxes. Dean was gone. Hanging on to his shirts wouldn't bring him back. They were finally finding a new purpose and a new life.

My Quilt

My design was perfect for me. I especially loved how the 54 blocks and strips represented the years we had shared.

My quilt would serve as the guinea pig to learn to use my new sewing machine and master machine piecing techniques. Hopefully, I'd weather and resolve any difficulties I encountered before I crafted the remaining quilts for my family.

Sooner than I imagined possible, I had all the blocks completed. **My creative juices flowed freely, and I lost all sense of time** as I played around arranging the blocks in a visually pleasing manner on my large vertical design wall.

My inner child, Lucinka, loved these times and eagerly came out to play. **I enjoyed rediscovering this long-neglected part of myself.** I was so close to completing this important milestone, and **celebrated** as I took photos with my iPhone to document this memorable step!

Perfectly Imperfect (or just doing my best)

Starting to sew the rows together raised a glaring reality I'd missed seeing earlier—multiple intersections where seams needed to meet *precisely* at either four or eight points!

To complicate this already difficult situation, the blocks had been cut from twenty-five shirts and seven pants—each made from different types of material. Some were sturdy and kept their shape when sewn to other block pieces, while others frayed easily and were awkward to attach.

I attempted different joining methods for days before I admitted how impossible it would be to achieve crisp points in so many locations. **I accepted that perfection wouldn't be possible, no matter how much I grasped for it. I needed to move on or this would be my Waterloo.**

The world wouldn't end. I could and would trade perfection for "just do my best" as my goal. What was perfection anyway but in the eye of the beholder? **Wouldn't just doing our best be all we can ask and expect of ourselves and others?**

Eventually, I got through all the challenges and completed joining the rows. **I'd done my best.** Renewed in spirit, I came through the other side much more self-confident. I took great delight in taking my first completed quilt top to Mary Ann to quilt for me. Before she started, she noticed the eight-point intersections so prevalent throughout it and complimented me on my work, saying, "I wouldn't have tried this myself!"

I still smile whenever I think of her comment.

DAN'S QUILT

Luckily, the design I had selected for my son-in-law was simple: a few long, randomly sized strips for each of the 21 rows. However, before I began, I double- and triple-checked all the remaining memory quilt designs to confirm there weren't any more bushwhack moments lying in wait for me. I was extremely relieved to find none.

After the strips were cut, I cast my attention to creating the final block arrangement. As I shuffled the strips on the vertical design wall, they'd fall off with the merest movement on any portion of it. Two folding tables from my shed provided the ideal solution: a *horizontal* design wall surface. **I was delighted with how that addition had significantly expanded my quilting project footprint into what had been the Radio Room.**

Taking my time and thoroughly enjoying myself, I built up the rows strip by strip, using a new-to-me method to sew the pieces in each row. Such **a welcomed respite** from the angst that my eight-point joins had created just a short while ago.

Perfectly Imperfect (or just doing my best)

Much later, I realized I hadn't cut some pieces perfectly along the straight grain, resulting in a slightly skewed strip pattern. I bit the bullet and accepted this imperfection in Dan's quilt. An interesting way to reinforce my earlier lesson on my "just do my best" mindset. I felt better when I remembered **the Amish made mistakes in their quilts on purpose because "only God is perfect."**

Dan's quilt turned out to be quite beautiful in its color and pattern arrangement and was **perfectly imperfect** in its final form. **I had done my best** and presented it to Dan, who expressed his gratitude for this reminder of Dean. He held the quilt folded against his chest during my visit as if he was absorbing comfort from these pieces of Dean sewn together with my love.

SONJA'S QUILT

I felt encouraged and boosted in confidence with two lap quilts pieced and quilted now in my DONE column. I moved on to my daughter's quilt.

Sonja is her father's daughter, a mini-Dean in personality and expression. Like the rest of us, Dean's severe brain injury and his final decline into dementia and death devastated her. My intent for Sonja's memory quilt was to present her with an in-your-face testament of her father's love for her. I also wanted to recognize her creative flair and impish and mischievous nature.

Trusting Myself and Remembering My Core Intention

The more I reviewed my selection for her, the more **I doubted myself.** This proved to be a significant testing point. When it came time to cut out the pieces and sew Sonja's quilt, I vacillated. I re-reviewed designs, investigated new ones, and calculated the material needed. I imagined the disappointment she'd feel with my paltry design choice. I'd second-guess myself and retreat to indecision. It was a loop without end.

This wouldn't do. I had four more quilts to complete and needed to keep progressing or I'd never meet my deadline to finish the quilts by Christmas.

Feeling desperate with the pressure of time marching on relentlessly, I grabbed a new design. It seemed simple but unique enough to rise above the ranks of *ordinary*. Thankfully, I had only sewn a few blocks before I knew this was *not* the pattern for Sonja. With limited excess material, I tried a few blocks in another design. This was another dismal failure in the *wow* factor.

I was now despairing that I would find the perfect pattern for Sonja and get back on the timeline I needed to achieve my Christmas goal.

Deciding to trust my first instinctive selection, I returned to the pieces I had already cut out for it. However, with the detours I had taken, there were no longer enough of the largest pieces left. **What was I going to do now?**

It took a while to stop panicking. When I eventually calmed down, I knew that:

◊ First I had to center myself and re-embrace my original intent for these quilts before moving forward.

◊ Then I needed to value and trust my intrinsic *knowing*. All I needed was within me. Believing in myself was enough. Trusting myself would simplify so much.

Perfectly Imperfect (or just doing my best)

I no longer had the largest pieces needed for Sonja's original quilt design. However, all each block required was a strip of additional material sufficient to bring it back to its original size. I knew there weren't enough pieces to match both the pattern and fabric exactly in all 42 blocks.

What else was possible?

Luckily, I had kept the extra shirt materials that hadn't been obviously useful but were too precious to throw away. From the stash of sleeve cuffs, shoulder plackets, pockets, and collars from each shirt, the shoulder plackets proved to be the lifesavers for Sonja's quilt.

While I couldn't get exact pattern matches for the replacements, I could match up enough fabric of a similar coloring to replace what was missing. With this new direction, I happily cut and sewed, delighting in the **perfect imperfection** of the solution.

The more I cut out and *sort of* matched materials, the more **I realized perfect imperfection is what life is all about. There is no perfection—only trying our best and doing so out of love. That is the beauty of the human spirit.** Everything else is chimera.

I laughed out loud when I realized this consistent thread was showing up yet AGAIN in my third quilt. That was a huge turning point. **All the delays and difficulties were of my own making because I hadn't trusted myself.**

I enjoyed recreating and rebuilding my blocks, and I'd start chuckling at odd moments, deciding how to best *sort-of* match the different blocks. My Lucinka loved this time of **coloring outside the lines.** This had been my biggest dilemma so far, although it was restorative and affirming as I came through the other side.

Divine Timing and Remembering My Core Intention

I started driving myself to complete Sonja's quilt top. My design detours had severely compromised my in-time-for-Christmas goal. I was finally back on track and only had three final rows to join together to complete her quilt top and get it to Mary Ann. That evening, I was getting tired, but pushed myself to finish it. **Get it done was front and center on my mind. Get it done for Christmas.**

As I guided the material toward the feed dogs (which advanced the fabric for the needle), a straight pin on the fabric immediately under the needle suddenly detached. It shot straight up into the air and then swan-dived down into the bowels of the sewing machine through an impossibly tiny opening. **The sewing machine stopped dead in its tracks.**

After recovering from my disbelief at having witnessed this impossible feat, I knew I had to find and remove the straight pin from inside the machine. Several frustrating hours later, I had done so and was relieved that things seemed to be back on track.

The machine lights and motor came back on, but no matter what I did, the feed dogs no longer moved. I researched and tried different solutions. Nothing worked. Time ticked on and my window of opportunity for completing Sonja's quilt top slowly vanished.

The comedy of events that followed in unsuccessfully trying to get my sewing machine repaired before the holidays was so obvious that I didn't take this delay as a death knell to my dream. I finally realized that distributing the memory quilts at Christmas would not happen.

I had strayed from my core mantra of **"just do my best"** and had substituted it with **"Get it done. Get it done. Get it done."** It was a hard lesson for me, but I finally accepted that **it wasn't my timing but Divine Timing that counted.**

When things fall apart and shatter our plans so thoroughly, all one can do is laugh and recognize **we can't control our way to solutions. Surrender and acceptance are the only ways.** With the "get it done" mental push shattered, I surrendered my personally set deadline. My new mantra was to **go with the flow** for the remaining quilts.

In the meantime, I switched my focus to enjoying the spirit of the holiday season. Our family enjoyed a lovely Christmas, made special by bringing and **celebrating** Wigilia (Christmas Eve) to the hospital room of my son-in-law Dan, who was dealing with chronic digestive issues.

We all enjoyed our Polish traditions, sharing opłatek (wafer) with family members and feasting on pierogi and other special homemade dishes. We shared our **joy and love** exuberantly (maybe even more so because of the setting and circumstances). **Everyone recognized and was so grateful for what was truly important in our lives. We knew the memory quilts would come when they came.**

When I presented Sonja with her memory quilt months later, she loved the unique and never-to-be-duplicated design. Funny how things work out.

Sal's Quilt

Sal entered this world in 2001—unique, creative, and distinctively artistic. Truly an original—with flair!

Trusting Myself and Perfectly Imperfect (or just doing my best)

I was especially determined to find the perfect design for my grandchild. Similar to Sonja's quilt, I dithered a bit but eventually trusted my intuition and went with my original decision—a wonky pattern of randomly-sized strip widths, dissected cross-wise in two random and skewed locations. Perfect!

This quilt top is currently in progress.

I've cut all the pieces out. Once again, the assemblage of "extra" material came to my rescue as I raided the collar stash to cut the final strips.

I've assembled portions of five blocks. But surprise! I haven't sewn any more pieces together for at least a month. The "Old Nagging Lucie" would have fretted and castigated me for my delay. But I trust that I'm exactly where I need to be and that everything will unfold in Divine Timing.

Sal recently visited, and I showed him my design and the blocks I've already sewn. I was delighted when he whole-heartedly approved and shared my excitement over its wonkiness. I know he'll enjoy Baca's (what he called his grandfather when he was little) well-remembered shirts in their new form crafted just for him.

Sam's Quilt

Sam is a family friend who currently lives with my daughter's family. Because of the enormous anticipation receiving one of Dean's memory quilts has been for everyone, I didn't want Sam to feel left out.

I decided to craft one for him but didn't have enough of Dean's shirt material left. After several visits to Goodwill, I purchased enough flannel shirts in Sam's favorite colors to make his laptop quilt.

I don't feel as much pressure sewing this quilt. I simply trust that working from a place of love and doing my best in crafting it will please him and provide him with years of enjoyment.

Maybe everything doesn't have to be difficult. And love always finds a way to bring a little comfort into people's lives through good intentions and actions.

Kit and Diana's Quilts

My son Kit and my daughter-in-law Diana are completely different individuals but so perfect for each other—with fundamental similarities interspersed with their completely distinct personalities (similar to Dean and myself).

Even though I have two different designs selected, they are in the same state of readiness: the pieces all cut out. The designs were easy to choose with hardly any dithering.

They'll be the last two I sew. Kit and Diana know this and have been *so* gracious in their gratitude and acceptance, recognizing they'll be the last to receive their quilts. **Their gifts of grace, gratitude, and acceptance** are so appreciated by me.

Reflections

I'm finding more connections from moments that initially seemed to stand alone. But then, one event or lesson builds on what came before, and suddenly **everything is connected.**

The memory quilts I'm crafting are a wonderful pictorial of all this. They serve as precious mementos of Dean, his life with us, and his love for us. They are all charged with my intentions for each recipient, the challenges and triumphs I've faced, and my inner growth while crafting them.

My latest repurposing of Dean's Radio Room is another instance of this. I'd grown tired of facing the brick wall as I sewed. It had served me well for three quilts, but I couldn't tolerate sewing there any longer. And I stopped just after starting Sal's quilt.

I couldn't return to that DARK corner once I'd enjoyed freely moving around the Radio Room, gazing outside at the beautiful LIGHT-filled natural setting streaming through the four floor-to-ceiling windows.

I knew there was a solution to my dilemma—my huge sewing machine cabinet, with its long extension and numerous drawers—languishing in the back bedroom at the other end of the house. I could position it in the center of the room to face those huge windows.

The cabinet would require at least two people to move it. *All I needed to do was to ask for help.*

I listened for days to my inner voice telling me, *Ask Kevin for help.* I thought, *That's too big an ask. What if he says 'no'?*

The message kept getting louder. *Ask Kevin for help. Ask Kevin For Help! ASK KEVIN FOR HELP!* until I couldn't ignore it.

I finally texted my neighbor Kevin to ask if this was something he might help me with. He responded quickly and it was done the next morning in less than an hour with the help of his friend! IN LESS THAN AN HOUR!

Life is truly glorious when we open ourselves to receiving help. I've always found great joy in giving. Now, I'm doing the same with the gift of receiving. And, since I don't want to deprive anyone of the experience of giving, I remind myself in those situations, today I'm the receiver.

I remember that same feeling of expansion and light in 2006 after Dean had been released from the hospital post-brain injury. I was so grateful he was alive and back home after all those months. It was a huge adjustment period for us as we carved out our new "normal."

His Radio Room had been transformed into our combined living room and bedroom—I slept on a futon, and Dean slept in a tented and zipped Posey bed. He was a 200-pound invalid who couldn't walk, talk, or feed himself, dependent on my constant care. I concentrated on doing all I could to help him regain as many of his abilities as possible, one day at a time.

THE FIRST CUTS ARE THE HARDEST

I taped get-well cards from friends and family that eventually covered all four of our floor-to-ceiling windows from top to bottom. Hundreds of them. Their quiet presence during this difficult time reminded me how much we were loved and supported. Gazing at them, remembering the love imbued in each, I regained strength to continue on.

I hadn't thought of the windows covered in cards for over a decade. These sweet memories remind me that this room I'm slowly making my own has—more than any other room in our house—shared so many of the defining moments in our two lives.

How appropriate that I've been drawn here to transform it yet again into what *I* now need while embracing all it has been. **And it's due to everything coming full circle for my turn at healing after a significant loss.** This room is now ostensibly mine, but I'm sure Dean is puttering around there as he's always done, just in a different form.

I'm looking forward to reacquainting myself with other memories long buried within these walls. And I eagerly await the next steps as I continue to grow into my future self.

I wish the same for you.

May your journey be full of life's delights and discoveries. May you embrace love and light to fill your soul. May you remember how magically AND quickly things can happen when we get out of our own way. May you remember that love truly is the most powerful force in the universe.

ABOUT LUCIE MIŁOSZ HASKINS, AUTHOR

Lucie Haskins is a lifelong student of how to live an expanded life full of freedom, integrity, and learning. As a result, she enjoys awakening others to what's possible in their lives and to the innate power we each have within us.

She's lived an eclectic life and career—first as a young Polish immigrant learning how to fit into a new culture in America to later experiencing life as a military wife, computer programmer, management consultant, freelance indexer and editor, and finally writer.

Her desire to share the wondrous information she absorbed in her travels, her various jobs, and her life experiences, went hand in hand with her thirst for deeply understanding all circumstances and information she's encountered in her 70+ years.

To that end, she's published numerous technical books and articles, along with facilitating workshops, webinars, and online training programs to explain the intricacies of software and processes for her audience. While she's no longer active in her technical pursuits, her thirst for knowledge and her curiosity have extended into writing about her personal life, most significantly the challenges and rewards of being her husband's caregiver in the last 14 years of their 50-year marriage. She is in the process of completing *Married Widow*, her story spanning the first significant years of her husband's brain injury, interspersing at-the-time news posts to friends and family with more recent reflections on her spiritual journey.

If Lucie's not outside enjoying the beauty and wonder of our world, you can find her head in a book as she absorbs whatever topic has aroused her interest and desire to explore.

RECONNECT WITH YOUR INNER COMPASS

by Libby Lee

I'm confused, lost, unfulfilled, and a little sad.

It's September 2011, and I'm sitting next to my son's cot, patting him to sleep. He's sick, and I'm worrying about my next shift at work. Why would I leave my sick baby to look after other sick people in my job at the local hospital?

This just doesn't make sense.

This turmoil is bigger than just today. It's my life in general! I'm feeling discontent with how I'm spending my time day to day as a mother, wife, in my career, and as a good human, craving to make a difference in the world.

Surely I'm meant to contribute more to the world than this work, eat, sleep cycle. Right?

Once I got really honest with myself, I recognised I wasn't truly happy, like deeply joyful and fulfilled. On the surface, no one could tell, but I had a deep, burning desire for more in life. I felt something shift in my body and couldn't deny it anymore. It was time to stop pretending that all was 'fine'.

That day ignited something in me. I decided there had to be a better way.

Do you remember a similar moment of realisation, followed by dread?

BEYOND THE SHIFT

You know, that moment when your heart sinks, your legs feel weak, and you realise you've been unconsciously fighting this off for so long, and now it has come to the surface.

There's no going back. You can't squash these thoughts down or sweep these feelings under the rug anymore!

It's time to face the music.

It's a point of no return.

Imagine you're on a boat, sailing through life on autopilot. The seas get rough and all you want to do is navigate to calmer waters.

There are two ways to do it.

1) You work through your process to change the course of your route. You plan, strategise, and coordinate your movements to get to safety.

2) You just turn the wheel a little to the left and hope for the best.

This translates to life when the seas feel a little rough and you know you need to make a change. You can either flip your world on its head and hope for the best, or you can use a process and create a strategy for what's needed to find your way back to calmer waters.

I call this "Navigating the Journey Back to Your True North".

My goal is to share some of my reflections with you in this chapter so that you too can navigate life along your own true north.

Storm in a Speedboat

I wasn't aware of it, but I'd been preparing for this moment for a long time— although I was going about it all wrong.

I think of life as a journey of sailing around the world. There are so many destinations to visit and different cultures to experience. Each one enriches your life in a different way and contributes to your own growth. If you ever feel lost, your intuition will guide you where to go next. Every moment creates self-discovery and new personal understanding. It's unending and ever expansive.

I realised that up to this point, instead of boarding the sailboat and heading off on life's long journey, I was jumping into speedboats, thinking they'd get me to the destinations faster. But they couldn't. They can't travel as far without refuelling. They can't handle stormy seas, and they were a distraction from the true cause of my mission.

My discontent had me jumping from one thing to the next, hoping to find the answer I was seeking, and every time I would find myself amidst another storm in a speedboat. When I finally got honest with myself, when that moment struck, when the seas got rough, I thought, "This has to change!"

Was I in denial? Yep! Utter denial!

And fear. Yes, lots of conscious and subconscious fear!

When you're in the middle of the storm and there's no going back, the only way out of it is to pass through it.

It was on that September day in 2011 I finally realised my 'storm in a speedboat' strategy had been holding me out of my true alignment for a long, long time. Instead of speeding up my journey, it was more like an anchor, keeping me stuck! And I would stay out of alignment until I found the courage to face the storm head-on, get really honest with myself, and make my way back to my own true north. Back to my authentic self.

Little did I know on that September day, I activated a new reality for myself that would take a few years to come to fruition. From that moment, the world began to look different. I felt like I was surrounded by possibilities and opportunities.

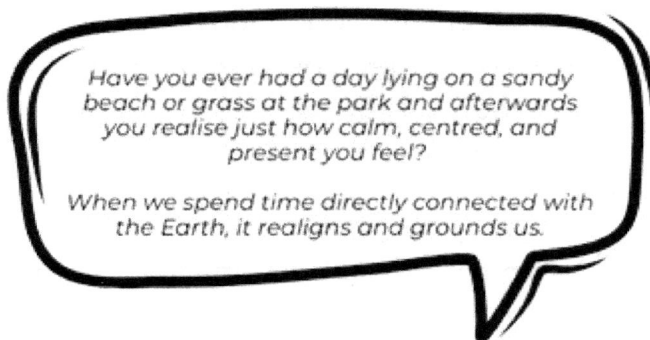

> *Have you ever had a day lying on a sandy beach or grass at the park and afterwards you realise just how calm, centred, and present you feel?*
>
> *When we spend time directly connected with the Earth, it realigns and grounds us.*

The spark that was ignited created a whole new pathway! It created a new yearning! A longing for a better way and to experience more in life. I knew it must be possible, and I just had to find it.

I recognised I had been on autopilot and had wandered off my path. I had compromised my values, looking for the quick fix or next thing, to find myself at a point where I wasn't living my ideal life anymore. It was no wonder I was feeling so discontent and unfulfilled.

I had done all the 'right' things:

◊ Worked hard since I was thirteen years old

◊ Went to university

◊ Completed two degrees

◊ Landed a 'good', secure government job

◊ Got married

◊ Bought a house

◊ Started a family

I'd accomplished the Great Aussie Dream!

So why did I still feel empty? Why wasn't I feeling fulfilled, if this is what life is all about? I had ticked all the boxes and done all the 'right' things. Where was the gap in my life?

THE AUTHENTIC ALIGNMENT

As we dive deeper here, I'd like to ask something of you. Regardless of your faith or religious background, I ask that you observe this next section with fresh eyes and an open heart. If it doesn't resonate with you, you can disregard it tomorrow. For today, let's see how this sits with you.

This image below is how I see us as humans, and it has a lot to do with why we can often feel discontented and unfulfilled.

We have a central energy source that all humans are connected to. It's like our sun—the centre of our solar system that gives energy to all parts of it. The same is true for humans connected to our own energy source. Some call it God, while others call it the Divine or something else. Throughout this chapter, we'll call it 'Source'.

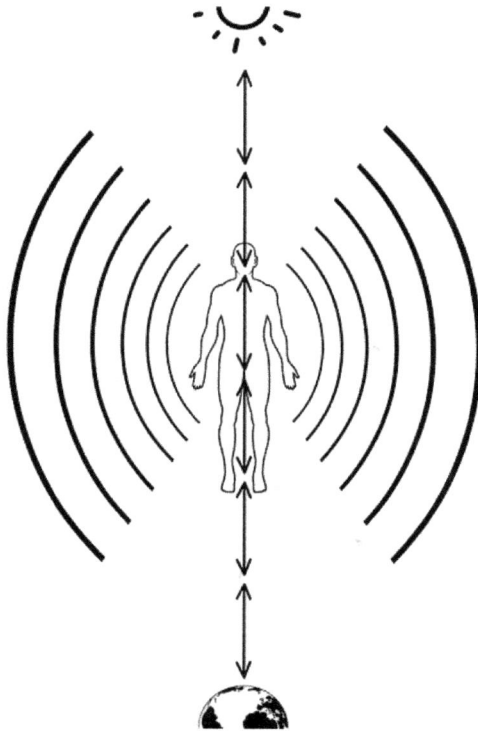

I believe the energy comes from this 'Source' through our human body and anchors into our planet Earth. So we are continuously connected to Source and connected to Earth.

This central line of energy connection (the dashed line down the middle) represents our authentic alignment. Our true north. Our calm waters. This is our unique connection line and is different for everyone. No two maps or journeys look the same. They each have their own code, blueprint, vibration, whatever you would like to call it. Just like a snow-flake or a fingerprint, they're all unique.

> **Have you ever had a moment like this?**
>
> *A time when you have a realisation or make a decision where you can feel something shift inside—and your outside world begins to change too?*

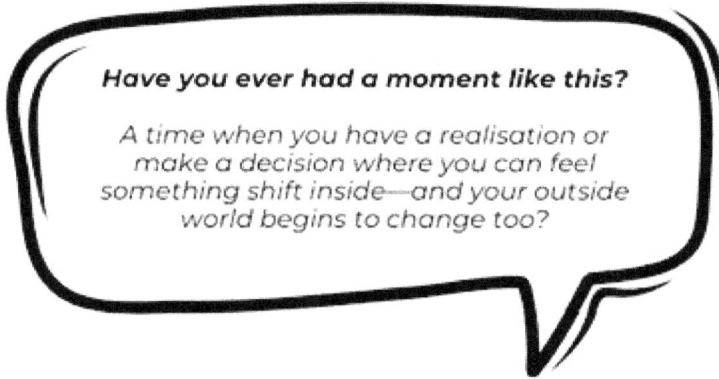

As little children, we mostly live each day along this one line in alignment with our true north, directly connected to Source and grounded to Earth. We express, play, and create whatever we are feeling at the time and whatever is true for us moment to moment.

As time passes and influences come in from parents, family, friends, and school, it begins to impact you, and you make adjustments to fit in. Usually, these influences create interferences, which are patterns or programming for setting behaviours to suit your environment.

These patterns aren't your truth. They are a compromise and a survival strategy. They aren't along your line of true north, so this creates an extra pathway (see the arc lines to the side). It feels like a shortcut. It feels easier just to divert off track for that moment to 'fit in' or 'keep the peace'. Yet, every time you are faced with those circumstances, you will divert off your true north and jump to your shortcut. The more you do it, that pathway grows and becomes very automatic. While you think you are taking the shortcuts or speedboats, you are really taking the long way round.

Each time you are faced with different circumstances that aren't in alignment with the path of your true north, a new shortcut is created.

Soon, you have so many shortcuts and spend so much time living your patterns and programming, that you barely live from your true north anymore. Until one day, your inner compass sets off the warning bells, and you pause long enough to see you have journeyed way off track.

Imagine all of the different areas in your life where you succumb to external patterns and programming to succeed, fit in, keep the peace, be liked, or stay safe. There are infinite shortcuts constantly pulling you offline from your true north.

Can anyone else tell you what your true north is? No way! This is your unique connection pathway and no one else truly knows.

So all those times you:

◊ Tell a white lie

◊ Ignore that gut feeling

◊ Say yes when you want to say no

◊ Put someone else's needs above your own

◊ Stay in a job you hate

◊ Stay in a relationship that's not serving you

◊ Compromise on your own values

◊ Do something you 'should' do rather than what you want to do

… and all the other things you do that you don't want to do, you are taking a shortcut. The more times you do it, the further from your true north you get. The more shortcuts you take, the stormier the seas become, and life gets hard. You aren't living in authentic alignment. Nothing flows well. It feels like you always have obstacles in your way. It feels like you have 'bad luck' or 'bad timing'. Sound familiar?

What it really means is you're offline from your true north. That gap you feel is your inner compass highlighting to you the space between where you are and where your own true north lies.

Our response to that gap or feeling of unfulfillment is usually to fill it with something. Anything! We generally seek and search for things to stuff into the gap (distractions, bad habits, etc.) to ease the discomfort. This was me jumping into speedboats looking for quick fixes and the next big thing.

For example, a person who desires success will fill any space in their calendar with tasks and activities to avoid the discomfort of empty time. Or, a person who's lonely will fill their time with dating apps, socialising, and casual relationships to fill the gap their ex left behind.

The common theme is that we will fill a gap with external resources just to soothe our discomfort. This is the Universal Law of Vacuum—an empty space will always be filled. If we aren't intentionally filling or closing the gap, the gap will be filled by the easiest option with the least resistance. That's why old patterns repeat. You may leave a relationship saying you'd never put up with that behaviour again. However, the same pattern shows up in your next relationship. Once we are aware of this and we use a strong intention, the Law of Vacuum will help us pull in what we truly desire and wish to experience.

What keeps you out of alignment and returning to the stormy seas? Fear!

It takes courage to reflect and realign your life.

When you come back into alignment, life flows with such ease and grace, and it's beautiful. You have lots of lucky synchronicities. Money flows to you easily, as if out of nowhere. Your relationships feel fulfilling and purposeful. You feel more passionate about your work in the world. Doesn't that sound divine?

When you are living life on speedboats in stormy seas, how can you close the gap and navigate back to your true north?

Engage Your Inner Compass!

I invite you to follow these three phases:
RECOGNISE | REFLECT | REALIGN

PHASE 1: The Journey Back To True North
RECOGNISE

It was time for me to stop long enough to recognise that something didn't feel right.

The beauty of being human is that we are always being given signs and signals of when we are on track and when we are off track.

Our mind-body-spirit system as a human is like an antenna system, constantly sharing invisible signals with us.

It's our inner compass.

It starts with little nudges, those subtle intuitive flashes or moments where we are shown that something isn't quite right.

Then the nudges become more obvious through our feelings. It's our feelings that really get our attention.

However, if we ignore our feelings long enough and don't make any adjustments, we can begin to suffer a physical ailment or illness.

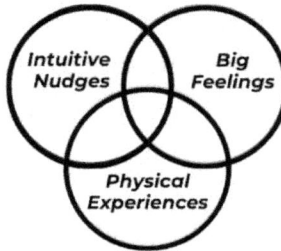

Intuitive Nudges:

You have a gut feeling you can't explain, or feel those bad vibes, and perhaps images flash in your imagination about how the event may play out.

Big Feelings:

You may experience feelings like dread, discontent, irritability (moody); irrational outbursts; emotional anger/crying; avoidance (numbing behaviour like drugs, alcohol, or any distraction).

<u>Physical Experiences:</u>

Aches, chronic pain, digestive issues, or even some severe illnesses can manifest in our physical body when we ignore the signs long enough. (Resource: "Anatomy of the Spirit" by Caroline Myss).

Have you ever had a bad gut feeling about going somewhere, ignored it, and then something negative happens? Like, you're invited to join a friend on a trip. You don't really want to go. It's an inconvenience. You have to juggle a few things around to make it. It's a destination you don't particularly like, and something about it just doesn't feel right. But you justify it by thinking you should be a good friend and not leave them in the lurch, so you decide to 'suck it up' and go. Then, once the trip happens, it's just a comedy of errors, mishaps, and misunderstandings the whole time and nothing flows well. Maybe those bad gut feelings shift into anxiety, and you start to feel sick to the stomach.

That's what happens when we ignore our initial nudges. All of that would have been avoided if we honoured the fact that our intuition was guiding us not to take the trip.

Or you find yourself in a toxic relationship. You're ignoring the fact that you're no longer compatible, but it's too scary to leave and be alone. You've ignored the nudges by pushing down the big feelings and trying to keep the peace. Then, suddenly, you develop chronic pain in your body that doesn't make any medical sense. Your inner compass 'antenna' is screaming at you to get your attention that something needs to change. You have taken too many shortcuts and ventured too far off course.

RECONNECT WITH YOUR INNER COMPASS

How do you get better at recognising the signs?

How can you train yourself to notice the signs when it's an intuitive nudge before becoming big feelings or a physical ailment?

Practice!

Take time each day to check in with yourself.

Take five minutes with your morning coffee or on your drive to work to gauge how you're feeling.

◊ Are you excited or feeling dread?

◊ Are you feeling proactive or procrastinating?

◊ What area of your life needs attention right now?

◊ Career, Money, Health, Romance, Relationships, Faith?

The more you check in with yourself, the easier you'll recognise when you're off track and not in alignment anymore. You're more likely to notice the intuitive nudges before they manifest into big emotional outbursts or physical ailments.

Referring back to me on that September day in 2011, I noticed I had feelings of discontent and dread around my job, and felt unfulfilled. This was my nudge. This was the signal from my inner compass telling me I was out of alignment and it was time to try to navigate back to my true north. But I'd been ignoring the smaller nudges for a long time. Every time I walked into my job with dread—it was a nudge.

I didn't know the next step, but I knew I had to do something.

So the search began! I was determined to make a shift in my life, even though I wasn't quite sure what needed to change.

I said yes to every opportunity that crossed my path. What better way to find what's missing in life than to test a few things out.

PHASE 2: The Journey Back to True North
REFLECT

In my reflection, I realised all the opportunities I was saying yes to were just for the money. They were good vehicles for making money, but didn't ignite any deep desire or passion in me. They had no heart.

If you don't pause and reflect, you will usually keep taking action in the same direction. You'll recognise that something needs to change but are not sure what that change is. You can keep changing and tweaking things but never end up landing into anything with purpose.

> **"**
> *"When you say yes to opportunities and experiences, you expand into a new version of yourself."*
>
> *~ Libby Lee*
> **"**

RECONNECT WITH YOUR INNER COMPASS

After sitting in reflection, I realised, deep down, I wanted to make a difference in the world, as well as generate income. I wasn't meant to speak on big stages, but I knew that I could have an impact, one person at a time. The truth is I already was every day. And I bet you do, too, in your own way. We impact people with how we show up in life. How we nurture a conversation or when we share a hug. One of the most powerful ways we can create impact is to show up authentically and speak our truth.

Something really magical happens when you let yourself speak your truth. It will repel the people who don't align with you and your values, and it will attract those who do, and you create ripple effects throughout humanity. Pretty cool, right?

This desire for impact is what attracted me to personal development. First, learning it, then sharing it by becoming a coach myself. I completed certifications in Strategic Intervention Coaching, Neuro-Associative Conditioning, NLP, Cognitive Behavioural Therapy, Human Needs Psychology, and Relationship Dynamics.

I have a strong desire to empower people, particularly women, to think differently. To recognise their own inner strength. For them to believe in themselves and reach big goals. This DOES fill my cup. I LOVE having a session with someone and seeing that spark in their eye when something really shifted deep within. You could see their whole dynamic shifting and it's so moving to be a part of.

This filled a bit more of the void than my previous ventures did and far more than my soul-destroying hospital job.

Coaching wasn't about making money; it was about making a difference, and little by little, I felt I was navigating a little closer to my own true north.

How do we get better at reflecting??

How can you be more purposeful and deliberate with your actions once you recognise something needs to change?

Practice!

When you have taken the time for your silent contemplation, and you RECOGNISE that there's an area in life where you're off course and want to navigate back to true alignment, ask yourself these three REFLECTION questions:

1. What part of this doesn't suit me anymore?

   E.g. If you feel restless in your job:

   Is it the location or environment? Is it the people? Is it the role itself? Is it the hours or workload? Try to get really specific.

2. Why doesn't this suit me anymore?

   Get to the deeper underlying layers.

   E.g. I've grown and changed. I've lost passion for it. I might just need a holiday or short time off. I may thrive more by transitioning to a different aspect of the same role. I may wish to advance or have more responsibility. I was kidding myself and never really enjoyed it.

3. What else is possible?

    What would you do if you weren't restricted by time, money, or resources? *This is one of the most powerful questions you can ever ask, as it creates a limitless moment of creation. Allow yourself to dream big and take note of the first things that pop into your mind.*

Reflecting on these three answers will begin to activate a deep knowing within you for navigating back to your true north alignment. This is where you start to close the gap.

Taking the pause to reflect on the areas of life that feel out of alignment and strategically making small (or significant) changes are how we grow and evolve as humans!

It takes courage! This process means you are leaning into uncertainty, and I take my hat off to you for your bravery.

PHASE 3: The Journey Back to True North
REALIGN

Before we dive into the bright, shiny, wonderful side of realignment, I want to take you on a detour and talk about THE CAUTION OF REALIGNMENT!

When I knew I wanted to make changes in my life's direction, I found myself stuck in the Gap Filling Cycle. I didn't like the discontent feeling, so I began searching for all the things to fill the gap and soothe myself. This was when I was jumping onto every speedboat and heading straight into the stormy sea.

Many gurus out there claim to know the secret to success and happiness. And I believed them.

I thought I had to be doing ALL of the things.

- ◊ 4am Wake Up for Daily Ritual.

- ◊ Meditate, Journal, Learn, Move, Nourish, Cold Exposure, Raise Your Vibration with Ecstatic Dance, Shouting Affirmations and Face Your Fear Challenge.

- ◊ Show Up Consistently (even when you don't feel like it).

- ◊ Always Provide More Value for Free.

- ◊ Hold Yourself Accountable.

It all sounds great, right? And it is! All these actions listed above are steps that can lead to huge success, but it's based on your INTENTION!

I was at the point of hiring coaches, paying them upwards of $20,000, and said, "Just tell me what to do, and I'll do it because I'm sick of this hamster wheel of lack!"

And so I did it all!

They said, "Wake up earlier." So I did.

They said, "Journal and write out your goals each morning." So I did.

They said, "Read ten pages of a book each day and learn something new." So I did.

They said, "Move your body through ecstatic dance." So I did.

They said, "Nourish your body with high vibe foods." So I did.

They said, "Have a cold shower every morning." So I did (sometimes).

They said, "Shout your affirmations, even better if in public." So I did.

They said, "Do a fear challenge every week." So I did.

The result of my *4am waking, cold showering, screaming banshee shouting, singing and dancing in public* habits?

Burn out! Absolute adrenal fatigue!

Was this my coach's fault? No! I believe his methods do work and bring people a lot of success. I believe to succeed, we need to constantly push our comfort zone and continually expand. However, it's not about what you do and what boxes you tick off your list. It's all about the intention you bring to each activity and doing the tasks that align with your values.

And me? Well, I had good intentions of wanting to create a positive impact in the world, and my approach to these daily tasks was as a shortcut, not as my purposeful path.

That's why some of my friends in the program absolutely rocked it and succeeded exponentially. Instead I burned out! They approached the tasks with vigour and prosperity. I didn't!

I was in hustle mode, and that's a big part of the narrative these days in most areas of life! The gurus and experts are telling you, "Be willing to do the hard things to create the life you desire."

Fair enough! It often works! The question is, for how long!?

For me: I was never enough. What I did was never enough!

If I missed a day or meditated for ten minutes instead of twenty, I would see it as a setback and a reason why I didn't hit my goal.

It became a measuring stick! It became a method of self-judgement instead of positive accountability.

I completely disempowered myself because I thought my mentor knew better, and this disconnected me from my mission altogether. I was so far out of true alignment that I was off the map!

How could it have been different?

Instead of wanting to fill the gap with activities, distractions, and external resources, I could have filled the gap from within.

If I was already aligned with the energy of success and I approached these tasks from this point, the story would have played out very differently.

I would have been fuelled and energised from these tasks rather than drained.

I would have been in ease and flow rather than living in resistance every day.

And the beautiful reflection I gained from this time in my life is that our body and intuition tell us EVERYTHING we need to know. I reconnected with my internal navigation system, my inner compass, that was nudging me and setting off alarm bells when I was off course and out of alignment.

Your authenticity is your true north.

As a collective, we have forgotten our own power. We've easily succumbed to the advertising and preaching of people we consider 'better' than us, and we give all our power to them. We swiftly and automatically put them on a pedestal while we abandon our own integrity.

"Whenever we place our happiness and peace in anything outside of ourselves, we'll inevitably feel unfulfilled and stuck." ~ Gabby Bernstein

Sure, you can take on advice or observe guidance from others. However, you learn not to embody it unless it aligns with your own true north.

REALIGN:

First, you recognised the stormy seas and the signals that were showing you you're out of alignment. Next, you reflected on the deeper issues underneath the surface and explored what else is possible. Now, to truly realign, you need to be brutally honest with what steps you take next.

Align before action.

BEYOND THE SHIFT

Take a moment to do this simple exercise as often as possible, especially before taking any action or making any decisions.

This is a beautiful process of self-connection, and I have recorded a guided journey for you to use, you can download it here: www.libbylee.com.au

Sit somewhere comfortable and take three deep, relaxing breaths.

Invite the essence of who you are to flood into your heart space.

Feel the presence and wholeness of you.

Use your imagination to see a golden string coming from the 'Source sun' down to the top of your head, through your whole body, out of your feet, and down into the centre of the Earth. Imagine that string is intact, whole, strong, and loving.

Take a moment to see how your body feels when it's connected to Source and Earth in this way. You may wish to take some more deep breaths and enjoy the moment.

Keep it simple.

When you're in true alignment, it is not about doing anything. It is simply about being.

The more often you come to this centred space of calm waters, the easier it gets, and you'll become more centred as you move through life.

RECONNECT WITH YOUR INNER COMPASS

Now that you're aligned with your true north, from here, you can make decisions and take action steps. The insights you get in this alignment are very different from what you'll get when rushing in the middle of a busy day.

Taking a little time for deliberate discernment and centring can change your life.

Now you can ask:

- ◊ What's my next step?

- ◊ What needs to change? How will it look?

- ◊ What needs to be removed?

- ◊ What do I need to add?

- ◊ Who do I need to let go?

- ◊ Who do I desire to meet?

- ◊ Anything else I need to know right now?

If you're looking for more clarity, you can use my LifeShift Matrix to assist you in finding your 'gap' and guide you to coming back to your own true north.

Dig deep, find the courage, be brave, and celebrate the fact that the awareness you allow in these next moments will accelerate your life towards your ideal experience.

LIFESHIFT MATRIX

Available at www.libbylee.com.au
Use the 1-10 scale to answer the questions below.

CAREER:

How fulfilled are you?

Are you in your ideal career right now?

Do you look forward to your work each day?

Do you feel warm inside for the impact you're contributing to through your work?

Total   /40 = _____%

INTIMATE RELATIONSHIP:

Are you in your ideal relationship right now?
Regardless of yes or no, how fulfilled are you?

If yes:
Do you feel secure that you and your partner can work through any obstacles you may face together?
Do you feel your communication is 100% open and honest?

Do you feel excited to dive deeper into intimacy with your partner?

Are you bored or feeling stagnant?

Do you feel you're able to fully give in this relationship?

Do you feel you're able to fully receive in this relationship?

Do you feel your partner fully sees you? Hears you? Understands the core you?

As a feminine energy do you feel you're able to nurture, support, and create in the relationship?

As a masculine energy, do you feel you're able to lead, make decisions, and protect in the relationship?

Total   /90 = _____%

MONEY:

How positive is your connection to money?

Do you feel like you have enough to live your ideal life?

Do you feel you can call in more money flow into your life?

Do you feel worthy of more money flowing to you?

Do you feel money in your life is transactional?

Do you feel you are paid what you're worth for the work you do in the world?

Total   /60 = _____%

HEALTH:

Do you feel you experience vitality?

Do you feel strong?

Do you feel aches/pains?

Do you feel connected to your physical body?

Do you have illnesses a few times a year?

Do you often wish you could change your weight or size?

Total   /60 = _____%

FAITH:

Do you feel connected to an invisible force or power (whatever you may call it)?

BEYOND THE SHIFT

Do you feel you have the power to create your reality?

Do you take time to nurture yourself and your connection to your invisible force?

Total   /30 = _____%

The area with the lowest percentage score is the primary area that needs your attention and focus right now.

Take some time to go through the three phases: Recognise, Reflect, and Realign and see the ripple effects move across all areas of your life.

For me, two of the most significant moments in life when I had gone through this process to get back to my true north, I realised:

> *I had a huge gap in my career:* The path I had taken led me to a workplace that was out of alignment with my values, and I became a version of myself that I really didn't like. Once I realised this, I plucked up the courage to leave my career. Despite the five years at university, the huge investment in my education, and the 'safe and secure' job with great income, I couldn't continue to show up every day.

I was bitter and angry, suffering physically, and gaining weight. I was in physical pain because I was ignoring the signals and my body was protesting. This also meant I wasn't being the mother I wanted to be.

Leaving that career opened me up to re-explore trading and investing, which I had studied years prior, and now I have the time and financial freedom I had desired since first having my son. I thought all of those shortcuts were going to get me where I wanted to be, but it was walking away completely that finally got me back into authentic alignment.

> *I had a huge gap in my marriage:* I subconsciously thought I was broken and that there was something wrong with me for not feeling able to be the wife my husband deserved. I knew I had more love inside, but couldn't seem to unlock it. We were 'fine'. We never fought. Our friends envied our relationship.

Once I was brave enough to witness the feelings of discontent I'd been hiding from, I realised I wasn't happy. I wasn't fulfilled, and it was time to part because fulfillment isn't found in another person. It can only be found within.

Once I recognised, reflected, and realigned these two areas of my life, I have returned to my true north, and the journey and readjusting are constant. However, the habit of using these steps to continually come back to my centre makes it easier every time. It's now painfully obvious when I am off track, so I don't seem to go too far anymore, and I've learned that the 'speedboat shortcuts' aren't shortcuts at all. A small gap feels huge and nudges me to recognise, reflect, and realign more promptly.

I wish for you to get to this point, too—where you're living in authentic alignment with your true north.

From my heart to yours,

Libby Lee

ABOUT LIBBY LEE, AUTHOR

Libby Lee is a visionary on a mission to empower people to align with their authenticity. With a profound passion for spiritual entrepreneurship, Libby has dedicated her life to helping luminous souls find clarity in their mission, ensuring they radiate their authentic light into the world.

With a wealth of experience and a deep understanding of the spiritual industry, Libby has become a trusted mentor for those who seek to create a meaningful impact on the lives of others. Her journey began with a thirst for knowledge and a desire to amplify the voices of spiritual entrepreneurs who were often overwhelmed and frustrated with sharing their gifts through business.

Libby's profound insights into the spiritual and personal development world have led her to understand the crucial role that authenticity plays in one's journey to self-discovery and empowerment. Her mission is to facilitate a deeper connection between spiritual business owners and their audience by helping them embrace and express their true selves through their work.

ABOUT LIBBY LEE, AUTHOR

In a world hungry for authentic and transformative voices, Libby has emerged as a beacon of light for spiritual entrepreneurs, illuminating the path to success and fulfillment in the business of empowering others.

www.libbylee.com.au

MAGICAL MOMENTS
FINDING THE SWEET SPOT IN THE POWER OF TELEPATHY BY HEATHER MIDDLER

I have always known I've been safe and protected, even as a little girl.

My dad was a single parent and raised me and my two sisters. My sisters left home when I was eight, and afterwards, I was usually alone from 6:30 in the morning until sometimes as late as 9:30 PM, especially in the summer months. Don't get me wrong, I had access to our community if I needed help with anything.

This being said, I had a lot of time on my own. Time to adventure and basically do whatever I wanted. Friends would often ask, "Isn't it scary being home alone, especially at night?"

I reassured them that being alone didn't scare me, as I always had an inner knowing that I was protected. I could feel it as a presence of sorts. As a little girl I didn't have the words or understanding to articulate what I was feeling. Today I would describe it as being divinely protected.

There are many times I look back on my life and realize how divinely protected and guided I really was. You could say I wasn't afraid of much, at least not until outward influences changed that for me. My dad always encouraged me and gave me the space to be me, but not everyone honoured me with that same grace. So over time it depleted my spark and dimmed my light little by little.

It wasn't until I had my first child that I realized that we all have a purpose, a purpose that lights us up and ignites the passion within. I found that when we do what we love and follow our Bliss, it's magical and effortless. She ignited that spark in her 20 short years here on earth because little did I know she was also going to guide me through my fear of death. It's been a journey to guide others through the process, making it a more graceful and beautiful experience.

Guiding others along their journeys of loss and grief through unconditional love with a nurturing approach is just that for me. Loss doesn't always have to be about death although it is a big part of it. It can be a loss of a relationship, job, pet, identity, and the list goes on. They are all significant and part of the grieving process.

One of mine started with my daughter's transition a month shy of her 20th birthday. She was born prematurely and had a life expectancy of 17 to 21 years of age, and with a double lung transplant, she was able to reach the 20-year mark.

I remember the experience like it was yesterday.

My daughter wasn't feeling well and asked me to drive her to the hospital because she didn't like ambulances. As a caregiver for 20 years, I wasn't paying attention to the signs. I guess you could say I was in caregiver mode, so I didn't see that this was going to be her last hospital visit. They called me into the room and told me she was at the end, and I needed to inform family and friends and start making plans to let her go.

They gave me a week to prepare.

It was very important to me that my daughter's wishes be fulfilled. She was intubated and sedated, so it made it a bit more challenging and unconventional but doable. It just meant I had to tap into my intuition. My higher self and her higher self would communicate, and then I would channel a message. I repeated what I received back to her, and she would nod yes or no responses.

I always respected and encouraged my daughter to make her own decisions regarding her medical care. I wasn't always the most confident person, but when it came to my children I was very confident. We came up with a game plan, and she knew it was that time. She had asked me permission to leave because she was so tired. We planned for her friends to come and say their farewells and then have one-on-one time for each family member. When her friends came into the room she was responsive and alert to what was going on because we planned it accordingly.

After everyone else had had their chance to visit and say goodbye it was my turn to go in. We had always climbed into bed with each other at the end of the day, especially when she was in the hospital. We would chat, play cards, watch movies, listen to music, share, and cuddle before we parted ways. I asked the nurse if I could climb into bed with her, and without hesitation, she made it happen. There was music playing in the background, and at this point, doubt started settling in.

"Am I making the right decision?"

"Is this really the end?"

At that moment the song "I Saw the Sign" came on and tears streamed down my face. This confirmed, YES, it was time, and this was my sign. I cuddled her and just shared time with her before heading back to my room.

As I settled in, I couldn't sleep, and words kept going through my mind. So I picked up my phone and started typing. Next thing I knew, I had written a poem. Again channelling from a conversation between my daughter's and my higher selves.

FROM BEGINNING TO END

From beginning to end
You've been there for me, my friend
I look at your journey while here on earth
There were many a moment, each with great worth
As you achieved hurdle after hurdle
I look at your life and it's come full circle
You did it with a smile on your face
Only you could do it with such grace
There were days when you had a tear
But really you showed no fear
For you always knew the plans God had for you
He was in your heart and in everything you'd do
To see all the lives you have touched
Knowing each one loved you so much
You have been a friend not only to me
But to everyone, that's easy to see

And knowing you're leaving
Keeps us all weeping
But now it's time to spread your wings
As we celebrate and your new journey begins
Knowing in our hearts you'll always be our friend
From beginning to end.

* * * * *

The next day, I had a conversation about organ donation. I was previously told we weren't able to donate, and then someone told me we were.

I told the administrator we would like to move forward with it.

They said, "We would have to postpone her transition by a day."

When I had a conversation with my daughter, she got upset. She said, "We had a deal, and this wasn't part of it. I agreed to this day, not that one."

She motioned to pull out her intubation tube to show me her intention.

Unfortunately, we had to cancel the transplant arrangements and follow through with her original plans. I respected her wishes and relayed her decision to the transplant team. They understood but were curious about how I was able to communicate that with her. I just motioned that we had a special connection.

The time had come to gather as a family and for her to start her transition. I lay in bed with her as they removed the machines and breathing tubes. I embraced her while the family gathered around the bedside. The grief at this point came in waves. I felt the moment her life force left her body and knew she was free from her struggle.

It was then that my life, as I knew it, would drastically change. Then, I heard my name being called in a gentle, nurturing tone. I looked up at the family surrounding me and answered "Yes" as though they were the ones who called my name.

They all looked at me and said, "No one here said anything."

That's when I knew something had shifted. My connection to the other side, God, Source, or however you want to look at it, had opened. I'm sure it had been there for many years, but my awareness was stronger now that my daughter had transitioned.

So many times, we disregard the signs and communication that are trying to guide us. We often brush it off as a coincidence when they're synchronicities to show us we are on the right path. These weird occurrences let us know when we're in alignment with our true essence and heart's desires. I frequently find myself saying, "Oh, that's weird."

The more I trusted the guidance, the smoother things would flow in my life. The moments I tried to do something "my way," the rockier things would get for me. Just this past December I was in that exact mode. I tried to do things on my own despite the guidance and signs that were trying to lead me. I was burning the candle at both ends so to speak, something I learned from being a single mom. It didn't work so well for me back then, and it definitely didn't in December, either.

With growth and awareness, I was able to navigate through it and recognize the pattern as it repeated itself. The circumstances led me to fall on my face, landing on my chin each time. Needless to say, it got my attention. I took a step back to process why this was happening. I was in resistance and felt stuck. My higher self was giving me the push I needed to move forward.

Often, we look at these circumstances and think, "Why me?" or "Why are bad things always happening to me?" When it's quite the opposite. They aren't happening "to you," but "for you." You just have to look deeper and find the meaning within it.

It's the inner guidance available to each of us that helped me navigate through the challenging moments and find the silver lining. I looked back on my time with my daughter with the same understanding and realized what a gift our life together was. Our journey allowed me to grow in ways I never thought possible or that I would ever dream of being capable of.

The biggest obstacle I had to overcome was the fear of death. I thought about how final it was, until I realized that was a false fear. I now know that it can be a beautiful, life-transforming moment. If you think about it, we all come in the same way, and we all leave the same way. It was something my daughter understood and shared when she was only four.

MAGICAL MOMENTS

One of my biggest fears has now become one of my greatest gifts.

Every journey is hard in its own unique way, although some are more challenging than others. If we come from love and compassion, we can overcome any obstacle. With the proper guidance and support, we can overcome any fear. The fear comes from the unknown because it's unfamiliar to us.

I have since guided many others to navigate through the fear of loss and other obstacles. Debunking it so it loses its power over us. Breaking it down into bite-size actions or understandings makes the goal more achievable, regardless of its nature.

After my daughter's transition, I was being wheeled out of the hospital by my niece because I was totally exhausted. As we exited the building, I blurted out, "333."

My niece asked, "Auntie, why did you say that?"

I didn't know I had said it, so I didn't have an answer.

We were searching for a hotel for the night, although there weren't many available as there was some kind of convention in town. Finally at our third stop we were able to find one that had enough rooms for everyone. When my sister registered, and when she returned to the vehicle she was teary-eyed.

We asked, "What happened? Why are you crying?"

She told us she got the three rooms and one of the room numbers was "333" which, of course, was on the third floor.

The three sisters stayed in room 333.

The following morning, we started our journey home. We were sharing stories and experiences we had had with my daughter. My nephew had shared how she liked to play cards with those who visited her in the hospital.

He said, "I don't know how she did it, but she always seemed to win. We usually played 21, and she always seemed to have a Jack."

Moments later, after sharing this memory, we had to stop for gas. He went to get out of the vehicle, but when my nephew looked down, he immediately got back in the vehicle. With some emotion, he said, "You're not going to believe what I saw when I opened my door. I just can't right now."

My sister got out of the vehicle to see what he was talking about. Two cards lay on the ground, one facing up and one facing down. The card face up was a Jack of Hearts, and no one wanted to see what the other card was. We all knew who was responsible for this, as my daughter's name also starts with the letter J. She was letting us know she was okay, and she continues to this day to show us signs that a part of her essence is still with us in everything we do.

Several months after guiding my dad on his transition journey, I had the pleasure of working with an elderly couple. They lived in the same building as my dad, and we had built a relationship over time. When an article about me being an End of Life Doula was in the local paper, she greeted me with the biggest hug and said, "You are going to do beautiful work in this world, and I couldn't imagine anyone more fit for the job."

Little did I know I was going to help her and her husband through the transition process shortly after he was diagnosed with cancer and was at his end stages. Our conversations started, first just in passing; then when they needed more support, I would meet them at the apartment. Her husband would give us space because she was the one who needed guidance. He was okay with his process, but she wasn't.

My guidance kicked in on another level when he was transferred to hospice. More questions came up, and her fear of being alone crept in. They were very close and did everything together, so that's where we focused. We continued our sessions through calls, as COVID restrictions had made in-person sessions impossible.

Then, the day came when she knew in her heart that he was ready to transition. She had lots of questions and feared what it looked like. I talked her through it, asking her if she was prepared to let him go, as I sensed he was holding on till she was ready to let go. She said she was and didn't want him to suffer. I guided her on what to expect over the next few days so there were no surprises and nothing to fear. When she was comfortable with the process, we ended the conversation. I also told her I would be doing a ritual where I spoke to his higher self. She was okay with that.

I had a conversation with her husband's higher self, reassuring him it was okay to go and that she wouldn't be alone.

That I would continue to guide and support her as she navigated through the grieving process.

The next morning she phoned me to let me know he had passed during the night. They had given him Tylenol at bedtime. He fell asleep and never woke up. She said it was very peaceful, and he didn't need any extra measures to keep him comfortable through the process. I asked how she felt about what just happened, she said, "I actually feel good and at peace." I could hear and feel that she really was at peace.

A few months had passed with regular check-ins, and at this point, I could meet with her in person. She liked that better because she would get hugs. Her next hurdle was going on her first holiday without her husband, as her daughter had invited her to come for a visit. I told her she shouldn't feel guilty about going and to embrace the offer.

I explained that anything she did from this point forward, her husband would be right there with her, experiencing all the things through her. So when she would go to hug her grandchildren, he would get to hug them, too. When she experiences things for the first time, he will also experience them. And if you stop living and enjoying life, they experience that, too. Our loved ones want us to live life to the fullest and enjoy every moment. They see and feel through us. Keep the connection alive. Even though their human suits have expired, their essence lives on.

Being present through the transitions of both my daughter and my dad gave me clarity and confidence to assist my Dad's neighbours and clients as an End of Life Doula.

MAGICAL MOMENTS

My dad's transition was probably one of my greatest moments. Heading into the hospital, he knew he wouldn't be returning home, so he stopped me. My dad looked me in the eye and said, "You shouldn't have to do this."

What he was trying to say to me was that no daughter should have to take care of their father like this. I reassured him it was a pleasure and an honour to be there for him in this capacity. He then said, "Well, I couldn't ask for a better co-pilot."

Being a nurse's aide for 20-plus years, taking care of other people's parents and grandparents, I set an intention that I wanted to care for him. He took care of me as a single parent and that was the least I could do for him in his time of need.

So, our journey began. Some moments were tough, and some were absolutely beautiful. His doctor transferred him into hospice, and I stayed in his room with him. I helped with his personal care and feedings, and I would leave occasionally for showers and meals. The staff told me he looked for me the whole time I was gone and settled when I came back.

Because of my dad's situation, the family knew his time was limited. My nephew decided to get married in his hospice room. They were really close, and my nephew wanted him to experience seeing him get married, so they facilitated it. He was so happy to be a part of this special day.

Everyone who could visit dropped by to see him. We even videoed a conversation he had with one of his grandsons. He received calls from family overseas and as far away as

Australia. Listening to them brought so much joy to his heart. He was a happy man, and his transition was peaceful. He definitely loved his family and was proud of every one of us.

On the last day, when he got his last pain medicine, he looked up at me and mouthed, "I love you." An hour later, I received a tap on the shoulder. It was my dad, and he said, "You can go home now kiddo."

I listened, and the room was silent. Sure enough he had passed. It was a very peaceful and tranquil moment.

Learning to trust my guidance has been a true blessing. Without it, I would never have experienced the beauty in all the journeys I had the pleasure of participating in. I am grateful for each and every one of them, and I look forward to being a part of many more.

My mission is to spread unconditional love, one conversation and one encounter at a time. To bring peace and tranquility to families during what can be one of the most difficult parts of our journey. Giving them beautiful memories that they can cherish forever.

Sending much love and blessings to those who find this. May your journey be peaceful and blessed.

ABOUT HEATHER MIDDLER, AUTHOR

I have known for 13 years that the telepathic experience I had with my daughter needed to be told. We knew her years on this planet were short, although it wasn't until the end of her life that it taught me to remember the gift of telepathy is within each of us.

My ability to tune into the connection between Souls is an incredible gift, and as an End of Life Doula, it gives me immense satisfaction to be with clients during this sensitive and emotional time of transition.

I often continue to work with people after their loved one has transitioned. I remind them that they also have access to communicate in this way with others. I hold this belief in their ability to telepathically connect to their loved one prior to death, through the transition, and afterwards, until they see and feel it for themselves. The relief people feel when they know their thoughts are received and experiences are shared through their higher mind and open heart is palpable.

You may reach me for assistance with your loved one's end-of-life transition at: hmiddler868@yahoo.com

ANGEL POWER
ENLIST THE HELP OF YOUR ANGELS TO CREATE PLAY, JOY, AND ABUNDANCE BY WENDY S. BURTON

Angel Power. Is there such a thing as Angel Power?

If you thought about it, could you go so far as to ask yourself, *are Angels real*? Have you ever seen one or felt one near you? Many have loved ones they converse with, whom they refer to as their Guardian Angels, but often, it is a one-way conversation. It is based on a feeling and a deep love for the one who has passed on.

What if we 'actually' have these spiritual beings beside us at all times, and all we need to do is connect with them on a deeper level? I remember thinking I wasn't sure I under- stood that concept. A deeper level means a time and space where all the chatter and noise of our world are put at bay for a short while as we sit quietly for a few moments and be with ourselves in silence.

Shut out all distractions and find a place where you can be alone. This is all that is required of you in the beginning. For those who enjoy meditation, this is similar to being still and quieting the mind. The only other requirement in meeting your Angels is to be open.

Our Angels are here to help guide, support, and love us. They want what we want. And if it is for our highest good, they will move heaven and earth to provide us with the very things that our heart desires.

I didn't always have this knowledge. Let me rephrase that.

I believe each of us has always had this knowledge from birth, but we forgot it along the way as we grew up. All events and childhood traumas in our many life experiences disconnect us from our true essence.

I have discovered that sharing our unique life stories gives the listener a frame of reference to relate to. How many times have you heard a story and knew something similar had happened to you, but you didn't think an Angel could have possibly been involved?

In sharing my personal story, I have, in return, heard countless similar stories. People have experiences of these benevolent beings who have transformed lives in miraculous ways that leave the listener in total awe.

When I first connected with my own Guardian Angel, I felt a weight lift from my shoulders that I had no idea I was carrying. From this point on, I promise you'll look at your life differently. It is my experience in life that we learn from examples.

I remember lying on the couch, trying to nap—even though my two boys were a little past the napping age. They were whiny and moody, and I was tired and needed a break. I called a time-out and made everyone go to their rooms so I could get a little space to myself.

I needed to shut off my brain and recharge, even though my mind never lets me have a moment of peace. There is constant chatter in my noggin, like an entire council telling me what to do and how to think.

ANGEL POWER

From my prone position on the couch, I stare up at the popcorn-stippled ceiling and silently wonder as tears trickle down my face and find lodging in my ears.

Is this truly all there is?

And yet, I know that statement isn't true somehow. I try to listen to the answer, and for the first time, I notice the voices are silent. *Great, now I need your input, and everyone disappears!*

I have this feeling in my soul that I'm supposed to do more with my life. Deep in my bones there's a knowing that I have a more significant calling in life than the one I am currently living.

There's no time to listen for the answer. I sit up, wipe the tears out of my ears, blow my nose, and do my best to put on a happy mommy face. It is time to check on the boys. I can't make them stay in their rooms forever just because their mother has another one of her 'lost' moments.

This was a recurring theme in my life, and each episode ended with me demanding the Universe send me my 'owner's manual'.

Then, one day, I had this shocking incident happen that made me sit down and say this can't be a coincidence. There clearly was divine intervention in this miraculous event, and I need to find a way to tap into this experience again.

Permit me to set the stage.

My boys are now living with their father in a town near my city, because they told me they miss their friends and hockey is better there. They are intuitive, and I wonder if they can see I'm struggling as a realtor and wisely bail from the lifeboat I am trying to provide.

I have always told my sons that wherever they are the happiest, I'll also be the happiest. This arrangement allowed them to choose freely without guilt or hurt feelings. Besides, their dad is a good provider. He's a solid role model, so I reluctantly tell them it's probably for the best, as it'll help me get my budding real estate career off the ground.

I drop them off at their father's and drive away in tears with the promise that I'll come and get them often for visits. If they can't leave because of hockey, I'll come and watch their games and take them out to dinner. It's a promise I keep, even though it takes every cent I own to do so. Yes, I am the epitome of the starving realtor.

It's the junior league playoffs, and the boys can't come home with me for the weekend. While talking to them on the phone the night before, I promise to come and watch their game the next day and take them out to lunch afterward.

However, in my guilt of not always having my boys with me, I have neglected to be responsible for my financial situation or even let them know I'm struggling. I currently have five dollars to my name, my car is on empty, and I have no idea how I'm going to go to their game and buy them lunch.

I cry and wail to the heavens to fix my situation because I'm a good person and don't know what I'm doing wrong.

ANGEL POWER

Please help me, Angels. Please. Please.

At that moment, I felt a calm come over me like I had never experienced before. As the feeling washed over me, I took a deep breath and decided just to let go. I've heard the saying, 'Let go and let God.' However, God was another word for the Universe, and honestly, at that stage in my life, I felt more comfortable thinking I had Angels instead.

Regardless of whatever my beliefs were, it was now out of my hands. I was letting go! Besides, I needed to go as time was running out, and I had two boys waiting for me on the other end. I handed all my worries over to my Angels; as far as I was concerned, it was now their problem, not mine.

Five dollars in gas would get me as far as the hockey arena in their town and back. So, with a newfound lightness of heart, I headed to the brand-new gas station just around the corner. I thanked my Angels for its proximity to my home, as I was pretty sure I wouldn't make it much further.

Pulling up to the pump, I grab the five dollars from my purse and head inside to the cash register. I feel embarrassed knowing they must think I'm off my dot for only putting such a small amount of gas in the tank. Feeling their judgement even before arriving at the till, I lowered my head and said, "I'd like to get five dollars on pump number four, please."

Before I could hand them my measly five-dollar bill, a loud bell rings inside the store, and I look up, thinking I've done something wrong. Surely, they don't draw attention to someone with only five dollars to their name.

I look at the lady behind the counter, and she speaks directly to me, "Congratulations! You are our one-hundredth customer!"

"I am?" *What does that mean?*

"Today, you are the lucky recipient of a full tank of gas! Plus, with our partner Kentucky Fried Chicken, you'll also receive a family-size bucket of chicken, with all the fixin's."

The lovely lady continues to tell me it comes with two side salads, french fries with biscuits and gravy, a two-litre Pepsi, and a chocolate cake!

Is this really happening?

She continued to inform me that the gas attendant standing next to her would now go out and fill my car with gas. The woman then handed me a coupon to go next door to the Kentucky Fried Chicken place and give them this certificate, and I could pick up my prize whenever I wanted.

"Can I go get it right now? I'm supposed to take my boys for lunch, and it would be cool to show up with a bucket of chicken."

"Of course, and again, congratulations! May we take a picture of you to commemorate this moment?"

She grabs the Polaroid camera from below the counter and takes my photo. The white image ejects from the camera, and my first thought was, *I wonder if it'll show my Angels.* I have no idea why I thought that, but I was sure they would be in the photo, too, because of the miracle they'd just delivered.

The lady shakes the developing image and blows on it, apparently to speed up the process. Before it is fully developed, she writes my name and 100th Customer in the white space below the picture.

"Thank you so much. You have no idea how much this means to me." I say as I take my coupon to head next door. Outside, I wave at the gas attendant, now washing my window, and let him know I'll be right back with my chicken.

My energy has shifted from feeling sad and depressed to joy and excitement. This is what a miracle can do. It can change your whole physiology in an instant. I decided I needed more miracles in my life. What a thrill seeing two little boys' faces light up when they discovered their mom had brought their favorite meal as a treat! Today, I got the Mom of the Year award.

Has anything like this ever happened to you?

Look back in your memory and recall when something so profound and exciting happened that it felt unexplainable. Did a loved one miraculously get healed from an incurable disease, or did a sibling survive a fall they shouldn't have? You found money when you needed it most, or that job you wanted more than anything, and they called and offered it to you out of the blue.

Miracles are happening all around us, but we discount them and chalk it up to synchronicity or just plain old good luck.

We tell ourselves and everyone who will listen, "We were at the right place at the right time." Sound familiar?

On my drive home after my gas station experience and a wonderful day with my boys, I felt deep down in my soul that someone had heard me that morning as I cried in despair.

I knew they would listen to me again if they heard me today. Something told me this wasn't a coincidence or a one-off miracle. *What if we could ask for little or sometimes big miracles all day long and actually watch them manifest?*

However, being the skeptic I am, I needed solid proof, and the only way I'd believe in miracles was with another miracle. But not just one—I wanted a lot of miracles! Several miracles would undoubtedly confirm that I had someone watching over me.

If I was going to ask for evidence of the existence of a higher-intelligent being, I needed to introduce myself and find out who they are. I couldn't wait to get started because I suspected I might be on to something here, and the possibilities were endless if what I suspected was true.

What followed over the next month blew my mind. I have a Guardian Angel! As I write this chapter, I want you to know my Guardian Angel and I have been communicating for the past thirty years.

What is truly exciting is that you do too! With the help of my Angel, we are here to help walk you through the steps so you can access your very own Angel, too.

I learned the first and most important step is to introduce yourself to your Angel and let your Angel know you are ready to meet.

Choose the best form of communication for you to connect with your Angel, and whatever you choose is perfect. You can do this by automatic writing, channeling, or meditating. Mine is journaling, which I've done for many years.

Sit quietly and make yourself comfortable but alert. Once you have quieted your mind, say the following aloud or to yourself. How you say it doesn't matter because your Angel will hear you.

"My dear Angel, I am ready to meet you, and I am open to your presence in my life. Please tell me your name."

Now sit and listen. In the silence, you will hear a name pop into your head. You'll think you just made it up. Ask the stillness, "Is your name…?" and you will get an affirmative answer. Congratulations, you have just learned your Angel's name.

It really is this simple. Get excited! Say hello and speak with your Angel. Know that your Angel is excited to finally talk to you, too.

#1 Introduce yourself to your Angel.

I told my Angel I needed proof. I heard her say, "Pick three things you would like from me that if I were to give them to you, you would know beyond a doubt that only I could have given them to you. Think long and hard and make the requests unique. Once you have asked, it is important that you get excited about its arrival. This is trust, and it lets me know you believe I'll manifest your desire."

I was clear on the instructions I received, and I also knew she wasn't saying I could ask for a million dollars. My intuition told me to go small but not so small that it felt insignificant. Her message told me to go big enough that it would surprise and delight me to receive this gift from the Universe.

I spent the next few days wandering around and looking at my world with a new set of eyes. What if I could ask for stuff and have my Angel provide for my existence? If this was a test, I knew I needed to make it unique enough that I would be shocked at its arrival and yet excited enough that I also would fully believe it was mine for the asking.

#2 Choose three things you want your Angel to manifest for you.

Make it complicated enough that when you receive these gifts, you know beyond a doubt that your Angel blessed you with this request.

I took several days to think about what I wanted and trusted the Universe to show me what would be exciting to me if it was mine to have or experience.

My first request popped into my head a few days later while vacuuming. I was listening to the music channel on my TV because that's what you used in my day when you didn't have a stereo. I'd just turned off the vacuum in my living room when I heard the most beautiful song playing on the

TV. "Your Love Amazes Me" by John Berry. Wow, this guy sings beautifully. I was in awe of this song and his voice.

That's it!! That's what I'll ask for! I want to see this man in concert up close and personal. Of course, I told my Angel the tickets needed to be gifted. They needed to be free, and I might as well make it VIP status seating.

Understand, I'd never heard of this guy until that very moment. I had no idea who he was or if he even did concerts. That wasn't my concern. That was my Angel's issue to work out without my input.

Boy, was I excited to see this fantastic singer perform. I did not doubt that I would get this opportunity in my life. I also had yet to determine when it would arrive, but I was confident if my Angel could produce a full tank of gas and a bucket of chicken, she could pull this off.

My first request, "I want to see John Berry in concert with VIP Tickets as a gift."

#3 Thank Your Angels!

This next step is just as important as the first two steps. Thank your Angels! Do you recall the last time you gave a gift to someone that was absolutely perfect? They loved it! They were so excited to get this present, and your heart was just as happy to see them accept this gift because you picked it out, especially for them. Often, the giver experiences just as much joy as the person receiving the gift. Your Angels love to see you happy and excited, so remember to praise and show gratitude to your Angels.

I was getting in the groove and liked this ability to use the universal shopping catalogue and my Angel as my very own personal shopper. So that night, as I prepared to meet my business partner for happy hour, I fussed around in my "boring mom" clothes closet and lamented over what to wear. I put on a pair of jeans that gapped at the waist as I hadn't yet altered them to fit my wide hips but cinched in my smaller waist. I'd wear a belt, but the loops didn't hold the belt properly when I sat down and puckered when I got up. In a bit of a disappointed fit, I took them off and decided on a different pair. I sat on the edge of the bed feeling tearful and asked my Angel for my second wish.

My second request, "I want a new pair of jeans that are so soft and comfortable, and they fit me perfectly in my hips AND my waist. I want them to feel like they were made just for me. The jeans, of course, must be free and brand new with all the tags still on them. I want them handed to me as a gift from a new person in my life."

Thank you, Angels!

As I prepared to head out that evening, my spirits lifted, and I was excited about the possibility of my second gift arriving. I knew it would be an early night as the house I lived in was up for sale, and tomorrow, I was hosting an Open House.

With the thought of a new pair of jeans in my future and free tickets to see John Berry in concert, I was determined to keep my work schedule from bringing me down.

All my friends were boating on a party boat the next day out on the lake, and I couldn't join them. From my vantage point looking down on the lake, I thought, *Wouldn't it be cool to have a telescope to watch all the happenings on the lake*? It would feel naughty but so fun to watch when I couldn't participate. Could I really ask for something that large and expensive? I reasoned that it didn't have to be new; it could be used, but it still had to be in the original box.

My third request, "A relatively new expensive high-end telescope, still in its original box, must be free and given to me as a gift."

Thank you, Angels!

OK, I had my three wishes. The next day, as I sat at my open house, I wrote them down in my journal to be sure I remembered all the details I had presented to my Angel.

Make sure you write them all down so you can cross-reference the details with the gift that arrives, especially if the request is unique.

Receiving my first request.

Three days later, my business partner called me excitedly and told me our client had given her two VIP tickets to see Michelle Wright in concert that evening. The owners of the tickets couldn't attend, so they gave the tickets to us if we wanted them.

With total excitement, I met my friend in the line-up for those who already had tickets at the VIP entrance. The two of us couldn't believe our luck, as Michelle Wright was a hot item in the Canadian music world, and seeing her up close and personal was such a thrill. She handed me my ticket as we waited in the line-up, and offhandedly, I asked, "Who's the opening band?"

"I have no idea. It's some guy named John Berry."

"Are you kidding me?" I asked her, gobsmacked!!!

Mentally, I replayed my request in my head. *I want to see John Berry in concert with VIP Tickets as a gift.* I stood rooted to the spot in total disbelief.

"Are you ok? Do you know who he is?" she asked, after seeing the startled look on my face.

I had to tell her. This was big! As we made our way to our seats, I shared my story of what happened with the boys, gas, and chicken. Then, I proceeded to share the conversations I was supposedly having with my very own Angel. I shared that I was to request three things to prove they are real.

Now here I am sitting at a John Berry concert with VIP seating, and the tickets were a gift *in less than three days*! And I reminded her that three days ago, I'd never heard of John Berry, but his music inspired me enough that I wanted to listen to him and make him my first wish.

I shared with my friend the other two wishes. Meanwhile, my brain was trying to convince me this was simply a coincidence. It was clearly a stroke of good luck.

ANGEL POWER

Seriously, what were the odds of something like this happening? Maybe they happen all the time, but we are too wrapped up in our worlds to pay attention to all the gifts our Angels provide.

As my brain justified this experience, I had an Ah-ha moment. This was why my Angel said I needed to ask for three things because she knew my brain would try to dismiss it as a one-off or a fluke. Brilliant!

I wasn't going to let that happen because I was excited—one wish down, two to go! I didn't care what anybody said, and that included my brain, which was trying to cause doubt and fear. My brain was protecting my ego by reminding me that if nothing else miraculous happened, I would undoubtedly look stupid in the eyes of my business partner and friends. Whenever fear and doubt crept into my thoughts, I consciously dismissed them.

I thanked my Angels that night after the concert for the wonderful gift and confirmed that I was excited to see how the others showed up. I had presents on the way, and **I believed**!

Receiving my second request.

While at the concert a few nights before, my friend also shared the exciting things happening in her world. Her daughter was arriving home from traveling in India, and she hadn't seen her in three years. And while she was away, she had had a baby and was bringing him home to meet his grandma. Needless to say, she was very excited and invited me over to meet her daughter and grandson.

237

BEYOND THE SHIFT

On numerous occasions, my friend insisted that her daughter and I would become fast friends. She had remarked several times that we were even the same size, so somehow, that meant we would like each other or could relate to our mutual weight issues. (I tried not to take offence.)

Sitting at her kitchen table drinking coffee, it thrilled me to meet this long-lost daughter I had heard so much about. I was stunned to see the slim, beautiful woman emerge from the bedroom. We were clearly different sizes! Only in my dreams did I wish to be built like this lovely woman.

The three of us sat at the kitchen table, listening to tales of far-off lands and experiences that left me in awe of this woman. With her backpacking trek across the globe, she had shed quite a bit of weight before and after her son was born. *Mental note—walking is the key to weight loss!*

Eventually, the conversation shifted to my Angels. My friend encouraged me to share my story of the John Berry tickets and my other two wishes that I was waiting to receive.

My friend's daughter was an attentive listener, but as my story ended, she got up from the table without a word and left the room. At first, I thought maybe I had offended her somehow. She returned a few moments later and handed me a brand-new pair of the softest jeans I had ever felt.

"I've been carrying these across India in my backpack for three years to bring them home to you," she said with a lovely smile on her face.

She told me she'd bought them for her trip, but once she arrived in India, it was frowned upon for women to wear pants, so she never got to wear them. They came in handy a few times as a pillow in the desert under a starlit sky, especially when she got pregnant. She had even used them a few times to change the baby's diaper when she needed a soft spot to do so. But for some reason, she could never get rid of them. She also didn't want to remove the tags because she felt they might be more valuable if she left them intact.

Of course, I offered to pay for them. "Didn't you say they needed to be handed to you as a gift? I don't think I want to go against your Angels!"

I went into the room and tried them on. Never, I repeat, never have I had a pair of jeans fit me so perfectly. I touched the tags still attached and felt the soft fabric, I couldn't believe how lovely these jeans felt on my body. It's incredible what an article of clothing can do to our mood. I never felt sexier than when I was wearing those beautiful jeans.

I kept those jeans for nearly twenty years before discarding them in a pile of rags. They were threadbare and had served their purpose. There wasn't ever a time when I put them on that I didn't think about how they were a gift from my Angel.

Thank you, Angels!

Receiving my third request.

This one took two full weeks to manifest, but after receiving my first two gifts so quickly, I admit I was starting to get worried. Looking back over the years, I can tell you everything happens to those who wait patiently. I do not doubt as I was testing my Angels, they were also testing me.

I was living in the interior of British Columbia, and my mother, who lived on the island, had just moved to a new house and invited me to visit. The timing felt perfect, as I had just sold a listing, so I felt relatively flush with cash.

While sitting in her living room drinking tea, the subject eventually came to my Angel story. Her husband was watching TV, so my mother suggested we move to the adjoining dining room so 'we girls' could talk freely without disturbing 'the man of the house.'

Whenever I shared my story, I would get excited about what this could mean for my future. Suppose I could tap into my Angels and show others how to reach theirs. Many a night, I would lie in bed dreaming of all the people in my life to whom I could bring this newfound happiness because this was pure happiness to me!

I had tapped into the Angel realm, and they had invited me to enjoy my heart's desires. Sharing this excitement with my mother, I got to the last wish, which I was sure would feel naughty in her eyes. A relatively new telescope, in perfect shape and still in its original box. "This gift," I shared with enthusiasm, "still hasn't manifested, but I'm pretty sure I'll be getting it soon."

A few moments later, my mother and I jumped as my stepfather dropped a box before me on the table, making our teacups rattle.

"Your mother bought me this for Christmas last year, but since she moved me to this house, the only thing I can look at is that lighthouse out there. And trust me, nothing is happening out there worth me looking at. These Angels of yours want you to have this. So, enjoy it!"

Sitting on the table before me was an almost new, very expensive telescope in its original but somewhat battered box! I jumped up and gave him a big hug, as he offhandedly said, "When you are finished 'gabbing', maybe you could show me how to see if I have these Angels too because I have a few wants of my own."

Thank you, Angels!

There it was. All three of my wishes were fulfilled.

They were unique enough that I knew beyond a shadow of a doubt that I would have received these precious gifts only if someone had listened to me as I made them.

Part of what makes this so extraordinarily special is my belief that it would happen—having that connection with my Angels and getting a clear message about what I needed to do left no room for doubt.

Thanking my Angels each time was the easiest of all. I have never been so profoundly grateful as when my Angels presented me with a specific gift I had asked for. I also admit it's become a bit of a game because I've come to love the extra little details present in the gifts I request. It makes it personal between me and my Angels.

BEYOND THE SHIFT

Over the years, I have helped countless individuals access their Angels with miraculous results. One friend of mine was so skeptical that she made an outrageous request to prove this was all bullocks.

"Ok, if these Angels are real, I lost my engagement ring two years ago while we were moving. Since then, we have moved twice. I want my engagement ring back! If your Angels are real, they should be able to do that, yes?"

I said, "If that is your request and if that happens, then you will know beyond a shadow of a doubt that you have Angels."

"Yup!"

Ten days later, she sent me a photograph of her engagement ring on her hand with the caption, 'Holy sh*t, I found it!'

She had decided to donate an old briefcase to a woman's charity, and as she was cleaning it out, her engagement ring was in one of the pocket sleeves.

Another friend was distraught over her dryer breaking down as she had no money to buy a new one. She called asking for help, and I gave her an idea. She requested that her dryer be okay, that it was very cheap to fix, and that whatever he said it cost, she could afford it. A few days later, the repair man gave her the news as he left her laundry room. "Ma'am, I was a few doors down on another repair, so I won't charge you for today's repair call. Your dryer is fine. A sock was stuck in the vent, causing it to overheat the unit."

ANGEL POWER

Over the past thirty years, I have leaned heavily on my Angel for all kinds of requests, like when I can't find my keys or an article of clothing. I even ask for help to find premium parking spaces. None of my friends are ever surprised when they arrive at an event and I have the best parking spot. I once asked for assurance I would make it home safely late at night on an empty gas tank. The number of times I've been upgraded to first class on an airline or won door prizes still shocks and delights me. I have won money without fail for the last twenty years if I attended a Superbowl party. The trick is that I always let my Angel pick the winning square.

In August 2023, I launched my first book, "Amy and the Angels" on Amazon. I can assure you that without my Angel's help in a thousand different ways, this book would not exist.

Please believe that your Angels want to communicate with you. Just trust that they aren't here to make this hard on us, and in fact, it's straightforward and easy. Just know in your heart all you need to do is sit in silence and feel the energy of your Angel surrounding you. As you ponder the reality of this moment, you'll slowly notice excitement welling up inside your being. This feeling is your sign that something miraculous is about to happen. So, get excited because, from this day forward, you will have a new friend who you'll discover was there all along. You just needed to be intro-duced.

ABOUT WENDY S. BURTON, AUTHOR

Hello there! I'm Wendy, and my calling is people are a "YES" to their dreams!

Being a published author is a dream fulfilled, and I plan to make this my new career calling. I am now a two-time author in 2023, with the publication of my first novel, Amy and the Angels. I only knew how to achieve this personal goal through what I have always done—enlist the help of my Angels.

I have journaled for most of my adult life, and to this day, I have a Tickle Trunk full of my memories over the past thirty years. Journaling has helped keep me centred and grounded.

Before starting my writing career, my passion for the (Paulownia) Empress Tree was the motivating force behind World Tree's immense success. I started World Tree as a "for-profit, for-good" company and advocate for the business philosophy individuals can create wealth while positively impacting the world.

My success with World Tree is something I attribute to enlisting the help of my Angels on a daily basis throughout that journey. When an opportunity presented itself for me to step away from my responsibilities, I took that freedom to honour a commitment I made to myself and completed the book I started so many years ago.

I live in a little hamlet called Sidney by the Sea on Vancouver Island. Above all else, I cherish my family and feel very blessed to have my children and grandsons all live nearby. Family night get-togethers playing card games are something they enjoy on weekends and special occasions. I will periodically call on my Angels to support a winning hand if the need arises.

I'd be thrilled to know your thoughts on Angels and if you enjoyed *Amy and The Angels*, available through my website.

Website: https://www.wendysburton.com
Instagram: https://www.instagram.com/wendy.s.burton

Author Photo Credit: Linda Mackie Creative

THE CRONE IN THE LABYRINTH
BY MICHELE WOODBURN

I am a seeker, with my own unique path through life and faith. I am also a Crone. My business philosophy is Spirit driven. My latest venture, The Labyrinth at Lavender Cottage, came into being from a desire to have a place where I could be alone and meditate in an outside space.

The path of a labyrinth is singular. One way in, the same way out. It is not a straight path but moves through bends and curves toward the center and away again before actually reaching the center. Much like life itself, it wanders. If I take the time to look within myself and look at where I am on the path, I realize I am constantly making progress.

A small town near where I once lived claims to have more churches per capita than any other city in the United States. It is in the Central Valley of California, a mini Bible belt. I resisted joining any of the churches, but found community in a youth fellowship, where I found listeners and wisdom. I learned to accept my Mother as she was and to understand our relationship better. The coping skills I learned still serve me today.

It is where I walked my first Labyrinth, which differs from a maze.

A maze is designed to confuse you, and the fun is in figuring the way out. A labyrinth has one path into the center, and the same path out again. Through the Church, I learned it was the path to God. From other resources, the path to the heart or womb of the Goddess. Either way, it was Holy. People reported healings and deeply profound experiences, and I felt prepared.

I was wrong.

As I entered and rounded the first turn, I realized how rapid my pace was, so I slowed and took some deep breaths. Rounding the second turn, I was shaking, and by the center spot, I was crying. Kneeling at the center, I stayed there weeping cleansing tears.

As I moved back through the turns, I met others walking inward, and every smile felt like acknowledgement. By the time I exited, I was completely hooked and knew I would build a labyrinth. I now view the labyrinth as an allegory of life itself.

As we walk our path, we approach the center or knowledge or the Divine. We can choose to spend time at the center, or move back out with our newly acquired insights. Life throws curves at us, yet we take the curve and keep walking, or turn around and return to center. Each turn or change of direction is a matter of making a choice. Since the labyrinth gave access to The Divine, each curve that life sent my way was like a conversation with Hecate at the crossroads.

"Which way will you go, dear?"

I learned to bring sorrows and problems to the labyrinth, and during my walk, a solution would present itself. This fed my spirit.

BEYOND THE SHIFT

As you journey through my life's labyrinth with me, I invite you to consider your twists and turns and where you are in your life on the path to Cronehood.

The Crone is the old woman past her "prime", which in our current patriarchal culture means no longer able to bear children. Our culture is youth oriented, and old is "undesirable". We need to reclaim the Crone, revalue our older women!

I did not recognize how conflicted my childhood was until middle age.

Doctors predicted that my mother could not have children, because she was born with Spina Bifida. Clearly a prediction that did not come true. She also had Bi-Polar Disorder, and I learned early to navigate emotional changes that could occur in minutes! All of this had a tremendous impact on my life, and matters because the attitude she passed on to us was that we could overcome any obstacle.

Playing outside as a child shaped me as I would come back home to ask my parents questions. I was not shy about asking, which led to my grandmother introducing me as precocious.

Two more bends in the labyrinth occurred as my heart broke at age three. I still remember the boy's name who blocked my way and told me, "No girls allowed!" I cried for hours. Many lifetimes of learning a difficult lesson came to me in that moment as one massive download, which has taken most of my life to understand. Being precocious didn't matter, nor what I learned or knew. All that mattered was that I was born a girl, and that closed the door to the universe. I want to be grateful for that moment, but I still struggle with the anger and unfairness of it and how pervasive the attitude is.

Then my parents divorced. Another bend in the labyrinth.

Every Sunday morning, I would get the paper and climb into bed with Mom. She would read the funnies to us and encouraged us to think and ask questions, no matter how bizarre.

Sometimes her answer was "let's find out", which meant a trip to the library, or diving into The World Book Encyclopedia. It was through our subscription to Jack and Jill magazine that we learned about the world and discovered Russian folktales like Baba Yaga. She is a witch who lives in a chicken-legged hut in the woods with her cat, and flies in a mortar, using the pestle as a rudder and sweeping away her tracks with her broom. She is depicted as imposing, ugly, and frightening, and I loved her!

As I dove deeper into her stories, I learned that underneath the Witch was an even older story of The Great Goddess. The more I got to know her, the more questions I had about why they portrayed Her as old and ugly. All the stories said she could appear as she wanted to, and there was wisdom and kindness in her quests. I spent hours in the library learning about her and how the Church—the boys—stripped Her of her power.

No girls allowed. Stay on the path.

Our father made no bones about his disappointment at having daughters and wanting sons to carry on the family name. Why couldn't girls carry on a name? His answer that I would someday marry and take my husband's name didn't satisfy me.

My mother said the best thing about daughters were the son-in-laws that they brought to the table. The interesting twist is that Mom encouraged us to ask questions and to do our own research rather than just accept answers. She taught us to reach beyond what girls usually did.

Take a turn in the labyrinth and walk toward the center.

My mother's illness sometimes resulted in her hospitalization, and our parents' divorce resulted in us being Wards of The Court. The same laws that protected animals governed our safety.

When a Mom can't care for her children, what do neighbors and friends do when presented with two little girls who need care? They take them to church—where I soaked up the lessons like a plant does water in the seven Churches and one Jewish Tabernacle we attended. It was water for my soul. I heard different versions of Bible stories, and I had questions, especially about the nature of God.

I loved that I had a Father in Heaven, but where was my Heavenly Mother? Mom never chose a faith path for us, but with her support, I would question, challenge, and search. I knew what I believed, and I was seeking a faith home. My challenge was that I could not find ME anywhere!

THE CRONE IN THE LABYRINTH

The whole Bible seemed to be a boys' club! I focused on Genesis chapter 1, verses 26–27. Then God said, "Let US make humankind in OUR image, according to OUR likeness; and let THEM have dominion over the fish of the sea, and over birds of the air, and over the cattle and over all the wild animals of the earth, and over every creeping thing that creeps upon the earth." Emphasis mine.

I saw myself there, hidden, buried deeply with Baba Yaga. The US meant the Divine was not just male—not just Father, but also Mother.

Why was the Church telling me that my place was only as a helpmate in the home? That I needed to be submissive to some man? There was no man telling my mother what to do, and I doubt my grandfathers would dare tell my grandmothers what to do!

Why was I expected to behave in certain, very uncharacteristic ways?

Mom stopped treatment and life became complicated with her bipolar cycles. She took the path of least resistance to divide and conquer and gave us the choice to be responsible for the housework or the yard work. I chose OUTSIDE and embraced my responsibility for the care of the gardens, the animals, and the insects. My interpretation of stewardship meant play with the dog, rescue a worm, or observe a bird or praying mantis.

This became one of the longer curves in my inner labyrinth, where I discovered my deep passion for nature.

One family who cared for us took us to their church program for girls. I embraced the lessons because there was a physical reward. I had a sash similar to the one I had in Girl Scouts, and for every lesson completed I earned something for my sash. I was not aware of it then, but I was being taught how to be "a good Christian girl". What became clear was that it conflicted with my sense of faith and fairness.

I had many questions about the love of God and how a loving father could treat sons, daughters, and people of other faiths and colors so differently. The idea that a loving father could send anyone to "Hell", where separation from him was the punishment, filled me not with fear, but with indignation. I was "Daddy's girl." Most of my earliest memories are with him. I now realize I was a depressed child after my Father left. I knew how it felt to be deprived of a Father's love, and could simply not imagine that a loving Father could withhold his love intentionally.

Meanwhile, my Mother violated all my sense of physical privacy once I hit Menarche. Instead of a ceremony or celebration of this Life Passage, she made it about her. She greeted me with tears of grief that her "little girl" was gone, and everything changed. Mom, who had been controlling but encouraging and supportive, now became accusatory and invasive. I longed for some private space to call my own.

Crying was both weaponized and a mark of weakness, and Mom cried often, and loudly. We were expected to know how to respond and do so immediately. If we cried, it meant that we knew we were wrong, and she won. So I stopped crying. One night, after everyone had gone to bed and I was crying under the covers, I felt someone sit on the bed and gently pull the covers down. A man I identified as Jesus/Yeshua was sitting on my bed. He opened his arms, and I moved to be embraced. Behind me, I could feel another presence that I knew to be Mother Mary with her hand on my back. After some time, I settled into sleep. I am convinced that this experience is why I live today and believe that I would have simply ceased to exist in this life that night. Instead, I felt profound Love, comfort, and peace beyond my ability to explain. I had been told many times that "God is Love", and in that moment I knew Divine Love. It was Life affirming and utterly inclusive and unconditional. My faith was solidified.

If we are created in the image of The One, are we not also a manifestation of The Holy?

I hold the conviction that the whole concept of God held by the Church is "manmade". God in a box. I hold the belief that Divinity is all gendered and ungendered. Omnipresent. Within and without. In me and around me. I believe that all the forms of all the Deities are simply different manifestations of The One.

I have a problem in that the word "God" is inherently male. HE is reflective more of the writer's time and beliefs than of a reality greater than words. This was intuitively what I felt and became more convinced of as I studied history and delved deeper into Bible study. I still walk "a Jesus path", but I simply cannot follow the teachings of the church.

Every tradition I have explored was created and ruled by men who imposed their rules on women. They silenced us in church and temple and made us "less than".

I knew I was not less than anyone. The unfairness of "a woman's place" as outlined by faith traditions was abhorrent to me. I still found wisdom and much comfort in the Bible, but I also found much of it to be the words of men and the times in which they were written.

When my Mother returned to college, she took us with her. I absorbed everything I heard and my grades reflected the knowledge gained in her classes. Then I discovered boys and a social life. When I brought a young man home and introduced him as my fiancé, my relationship with my mother became increasingly hostile.

A confrontation with her caused me to move in with a friend with just the clothes on my back. My fiancé and I began hunting for an apartment. We earned decent money and had planned a big wedding, but chose to go to the courthouse.

I was approaching the next turn.

Getting pregnant back in 1970 was enough to make me "unemployable". Then my husband quit his job and took up panhandling. He would leave early each day to look for work. A phone call from an outraged friend revealed that his actual destination was his girlfriend's house. I filed for divorce and was alone with my daughter.

We learned to make our own fun, and I wanted wholesome activities to encourage my daughter to grow wings. I enrolled her in Girl Scouting, and I became the Troop Leader. The church that sponsored us was gracious and welcoming, and I found a new way to explore my faith. My new community offered a women's organization where womanhood and a woman's "place" were topics for discussion and debate.

This congregation supported each other and, for me, that came as a job offer. I had questioned the ethics of "selling", and the offer allowed me to use my retail experience and training in "service" as a teacher.

This felt like a turn to the center of the labyrinth.

The new job involved training housewives and immigrants for jobs in retail. As I taught them percentages and how to merchandise a shelf, they taught me about life. After the wave of Hmong immigrants following the end of the Vietnam War, I learned about Hmong culture. One of the most important things I learned was to watch their faces for understanding. In their culture, a teacher is important, and a lack of understanding is a failure on the part of the student, never a reflection of the teacher's ability to relate the material.

In reality, I was performing a service in "selling". At the point of placement, I had to sell each student to a prospective employer.

When the state of California hit a budget crisis, my program closed, and they moved me to another program, along with four other women. It was my first encounter with The Sister Wound. The women I began working with did not want me there. It was not in any way a pleasant working environment. I went to my Pastor, who referred me to a counselor but never treated me the same. Suddenly I stopped being seen as a strong, capable professional, and became a poor little woman who needed help.

Turn away from the center.

My church used a portable labyrinth, and I walked that labyrinth regularly, but longed for one that did not smell like plastic. My desire to build my own labyrinth was revived.

The Church was teaching me that I could not expect to feel complete until I found a husband. Life revealed my standards were going to be difficult for most men to achieve. In college, I learned about insecure attachment as a child and how that had affected my development. I began to believe I might be entitled to think well of myself and my achievements, and was viewing the world around me without the fear that others had taught me. Fear never sat well with me, and I now saw how it had governed me.

When my office and program closed, the agency I worked for offered me a job that paid minimum wage. I knew I was worth more, and my response was, "No, thank you."

I returned to college on a full-time basis. I focused on the required courses, including a PE course I had been avoiding.

When I was in grade school, the nurse made the rounds of each class to measure our height and weight, and called them out for the teacher to record. I was behind a classmate, and when her weight was called, there was an audible gasp. When my weight was called, I was the one who gasped. I weighed as much as she did, and she was FAT! I was very muscular, but didn't know that muscle weighs more than fat. My self image plummeted.

THE CRONE IN THE LABYRINTH

I was mortified in grade six when I developed young and needed a bra, and then failed the annual eye test and needed glasses. The gregarious, confident little girl became withdrawn.

My insecurities in my appearance and sense of belonging hit bottom. The mean girls in middle school made sure I knew I wasn't cool and doomed because no boy would ever look twice at me. We also had to take "Gym" in middle school, which meant changing into dreaded dark blue shorts and a white blouse that traitorously refused to stay snapped.

We had to line up for roll call and were to answer "Present" and call out the day of our menses. They assigned girls who were menstruating to a private shower stall and changing room. A teacher followed me in to see if I was lying! Imagine my humiliation!

All of this contributed to an intense dislike of PE classes which followed me all the way to college, where I tried every argument I could think of to get out of it! My counselor was undeterred. She pointed out that I had options to choose from, and I finally selected one euphemistically titled "Personal Fitness". It was primarily a weightlifting class.

After Introductions to the equipment and safe usage of each, they measured us for Body Mass Index or BMI. I don't remember what mine was—that fell too squarely into my self-loathing morass. All I remember is my gratitude to the man who took the measurement and recorded it silently.

It turns out weightlifting is my jam! I loved the class! I learned about the difference between fat and muscle, and started feeling good about working out. In an atmosphere which is usually predominantly male, I was blossoming. I was having fun in a PE class!

My daughter was graduating from high school at the same time I was going to graduate from college. I started doing research to move to Germany—my maternal ancestral home. I wanted a clean slate!

One of my gym instructors, Erin, was knowledgeable about many subjects. We discussed my plans to move to Germany. He was a Highland Games athlete and gave me support and encouragement. When I found out he was participating in a nearby event, I invited myself to come watch.

I had not dated in years. After my divorce, I realized I was looking for someone who I could actually converse with. The men I was meeting were interested in sex. Not that I wasn't, but I had requirements. Then there was that "chemistry" thing that makes the heart beat faster and adrenaline rush through the system.

When Erin turned around at that event, his face lit up, and I felt that flush of adrenaline. I started timing my workouts for when he supervised the weight room. When he told me the college was hosting a Track and Field event and he was in charge, I volunteered to help. As a thank you, his habit was to provide dinner. I slipped him a note with my phone number and instructions not to lose it so I could claim my dinner. He kept the note.

We were married three months later, and I finally got my big wedding. I did not move to Germany, but we went to

Germany for Eisstockschießen or Ice Stock, which is similar to curling. We joined the US team and fielded both a men's and women's team at the World Championships. I want to tell you how we were a committed and plucky bunch, but the more honest goal was to not come in dead last, which we didn't. Full disclosure, the Swiss team had too many players on the ice and lost by forfeit! We took the win!

After the tournament we had a week to tour. One of our stops was Dachau.

The prison camp in Dachau is small and surrounded by the city. The camp is ringed by a chain-link fence and busy streets on all sides. As we entered, we were presented with artifacts from the camp and large pictures of the prisoners and activities in the camp. Around us we could hear conversations in shocked tones.

Our first sight was a black metal sculpture of fence posts, barbed wire, and emaciated human figures and skeletons that almost floated in the barbed wire. Contorted figures portrayed the agony suffered by inmates there. The sculpture was made and designed by Nandor Glid, a Yugoslavian artist and concentration camp survivor. The work depicts the people who flung themselves onto the barbed wire, or attempted to climb it, and were shot by the SS. All conversation suddenly ceased.

After this, any speaking was in whispers. As we walked through the camp, the absence of any noise struck me. The traffic, which had been heavy, made no sound inside. Birds did not enter, although they had been singing as we walked along the outside of the fence. Even weeds did not seem to want to grow inside the grounds. Dachau was the first of Hitler's concentration camps. A work camp.

Proclaimed by the sign over the original entry gate which read "Arbeit Macht Frei". Literally, work makes free, or freedom through work. It was the model and training site for the other camps, and for over 40,000 people, a place of death.

I spotted a sign with an arrow that directed us to a "Healing Garden" at the back of the camp. We were alone there. After the horror still palpable in the camp, this felt different. I stopped to read a poem and declaration that urged that we never forget lest we doom ourselves to repeat this. It was beautiful and signed by every faith and religion, and spoke of the triumph of Love over Evil. The sense of the power of Love in that place broke me.

Almost 30 years after that experience, I cannot speak or write about it without tears. It was not the absolute horror of the place that affected me most, although I will never forget it. The most lasting impact on me was the Power of Love and the universality of the declaration. In that most evil of places, I was in the presence of The Holy and it was a power beyond description.

Because Erin listened and supported me without suggesting solutions, I learned to make my own choices and decisions. I started my business, and the services I had been offered minimum wage for, I now offered as an agency. We also started a family.

THE CRONE IN THE LABYRINTH

What interested me most were women's issues, especially relative to employment, cultural context, and spirituality. I had questions about the Divine Feminine and wanted to grow spiritually. To understand myself and grow past the experiences of my maidenhood.

My faith and spiritual beliefs were powerful motivators, even in my business. I started examining the milestones in my life and how they had been celebrated or not. Women held ceremonies for young women, whereas in my home, we met the transition to maidenhood with weeping, grief, distrust, and suspicion. I felt shame and loathing during my periods.

As a young mother, I banked breast milk, and switched to cloth pads and an enamel rinse tub during my periods. I offered my blood to my garden, although I made offerings at night, aware of the possibility that I might offend others. Clearly my garden loved this! I instinctively felt it was right to perform these celebrations of womanhood.

I discovered and explored Wicca, and ran head on into the Wiccan Rede.

The fear that ruled my Mother taught me to be afraid of casting a circle or performing a spell and leaving myself vulnerable. I knew I could not raise the perfection when called to "bind the wiccan rede ye must, in perfect love and perfect trust".

My first Witch came along at the same time as my second husband. She was young, smart, and beautiful, and encouraged me to continue my research. She provided me with a wish bottle that I still have.

When I asked a Pastor about Exodus 22:18, "Thou shalt not suffer a Witch to live", the explanation was that witchcraft was a sin. I was suspicious that the writer of the verse perceived witchcraft as a threat to his power or authority.

Later, when I asked another Pastor in another congregation the same question, he shrugged and said, "I don't know, he must have thought she was a threat." Subject closed.

My new husband did not share my faith, feeling that all religion was a method of controlling people. While I tried to understand his viewpoint, what I experienced viscerally was fear. I feared that the Church might be right, and death would separate us.

As I explored my fear of losing him, I saw clearly how the writers of the Bible and the church itself had used fear to control us. They had demonized other cultures and religions prevalent in the places that the Hebrew armies had invaded and conquered. It is a tactic commonly employed to dehumanize an enemy or culture in order to convince people to do battle with the enemy. If "the other" is seen as evil or subhuman, it becomes acceptable to kill them and destroy the culture.

This recognition of an ancient patriarchal tactic led me to revisit my fear of witchcraft. My continued exploration of witchcraft had shown me a world of ideas that resonated more with my personal beliefs than what the Church was offering. The books I read contained more love and acceptance than what I was finding in church. Jesus spoke of love, and obviously respected women, but other biblical writers seemed to follow a different philosophy.

THE CRONE IN THE LABYRINTH

Where were the stories of women and the writings of women? I shifted deeper into the feminist zone.

Another bend in the labyrinth came when my son was born.

A friend raised with practices and ceremonies helped me to celebrate and recover from the birth with simple ceremonies, special foods, and herbs. The experience was powerful and healing to my soul. I could celebrate the power of the whole experience.

Ceremony makes all the difference!

When it became clear that I was approaching menopause, I started researching the aging process and found *Goddesses in Everywoman* and *Crones Don't Whine* by Jean Shinoda Bolen. I saw myself and realized I had issues with some of the Goddess archetypes.

When God Was A Woman by Merlin Stone validated my sense of being "cut out".

Goddesses in Older Women by Jean Shinoda Bolen helped me realize that, while I wasn't fully a Crone, I liked the older goddesses much better! It was a homecoming, since my first love had been Baba Yaga. I understood much more clearly how suppressed She had been.

I discovered the 13 Moon Mystery School, where we explored the strengths and shadows of each archetype and how those manifested within us. I no longer had "issues" with any particular Goddess, only greater or lesser influence on me.

I met other Witches and Priestesses during my explorations of The Mother Wound, The Sister Wound, and The Witch Wound. I had found my spirit home and moved beyond the Wiccan tradition. I was finally free from the fear of damnation, instilled hundreds of years ago by the Witch hunts and trials.

I could pursue a spiritual path that actually celebrated me as a woman! Stepping into my power after a lifetime of being told that I should be obedient was frightening and liberating at the same time.

This was the why of Exodus 22:18! A woman with power could not be controlled! Would not be controlled. The unfairness of "no girls allowed" followed me throughout my life—the "boy's club" in church, medical settings, work, and school.

As a young maiden and mother, I desired the protection and companionship of a man who would honor me. I was not willing to settle for less. Although I held feminist views, I also desired to be accepted and successful in my career. It was galling to present my ideas through the voice of a man so they would be heard, but I was willing to do that in order to be successful.

With experience, I recognized I had donned a mask that hid the real me from view. Respectability. Professionalism. Choose a name. I accepted my role as less than, despite my conviction that I was important. Precocious. And very capable.

In the United States, we are unraveling our status as conquerors and colonizers, our white supremacy and privilege. We are opening our eyes to gender stereotypes. I saw my spiritual beliefs and the reality of what my church was professing through these lenses. When the Methodist Church voted to ban LGBTQIA+ clergy and marriage, I was done.

Gathering in a community, which had been important to me, was no longer an option when COVID hit. It was the time to go within, to more deeply explore my faith and spiritual beliefs. I found my community online.

Another turn in towards the center.

The last two ministers assigned to my congregation were women. The first saw people leave the Church, refusing to be led by a woman. The first toe in the water feels the chill. She mentioned the Biblical names for God that embraced the feminine and deferred to me for the Pagan origins of church holidays. Our congregation was being educated, and thousands of years of editing and rewriting by men was being at least slightly unraveled. She spoke of the myriad Celtic names for Divinity, many of which began "Mother of...".

Everything happens in Divine timing.

Prior to the Pandemic, I traveled with my 13 Moon Priestess to a retreat in Ireland, which is my Paternal ancestral home. Our focus was Brigid, one of the three Irish Patron Saints, who is still viewed as The Goddess. The Catholic Church appropriated the Goddess Brigid but changed her story, because she could not be fully repressed. She is alive and present in Ireland, as is The Cailleach, the Crone.

During the retreat, we had a Croning ceremony for me. They asked me why this was important.

I was ready!

A woman living in the past did not have the options available to us today. The laws that governed them took away all their rights and property when they lost their husband, regardless of their age. If a son were to take her in, she could live out her life as help in his home. If she had only daughters or no children or young children, she was forced to make her way with nothing and branded as "carogne" or carrion. Forced to live as if already dead, with no value, no power, invisible except to receive insult or injury. If she dared to make a small living by selling herbs, or making medicines, she could be accused of Witchcraft and her life put at risk.

My own Grandmothers were both good examples of Crones. These women spoke their minds plainly and clearly, and anyone attempting to silence them would be in for a rough ride!

ALL women should be able to embrace that kind of wisdom and power! Ceremonially becoming a Crone matters as a recognition of a life passage, and to reclaim the honor and power due to our elder women!

We need the Crone to offer the perspective of looking back at life, and the joys of actually being older. To share wisdom. The age at which one becomes a Crone is highly individual. I was 63 when I was Croned, but I believe a woman past fifty has earned the right to the title.

I have an issue with a woman younger than fifty claiming Cronehood. Before that age, she is still in the Mother era. With many women choosing not to bear children now, or unable to bear children, there are objections to being called "Mother". I have heard suggestions for adding a fourth face, Maiden, Mother, Queen, and Crone, but ALL women are Queens, regardless of stage of life. The movement to add a fourth face is a form of acquiescence to patriarchal programming. We do not need to produce children ourselves to be the Mothers of culture and society.

Crone is said to denigrate women. Its word origin is Old French, and it comes from the same root as the term carrion. The word "hag" is a derivation of an old English or Proto-Germanic word and meant "repulsive old woman" or "Witch". A woman living without a place to bathe, change, or otherwise provide comfort may indeed have been repulsive. One can see how the picture of the repulsive old Witch is drawn by a system invested in maintaining itself.

Aging is not always comfortable, and people still fear the loss of youth.

A book by Etta Clark, *Growing Old is Not For Sissies: Portraits of Senior Athletes* made a tremendous impact on me. Aging could be wonderful.

The Croning ceremony was important for many reasons. Women have benefitted from changing laws that no longer dispossess us. We still carry the patriarchal programming that makes us less than the male members of our societies. Both of my Grandmothers ran their households, and both Grandfathers dutifully turned over paychecks. I run ours, including money management and bill paying. My husband's name and social security number remain first on our bills and taxes. I memorized my husband's social security number to conduct business.

Women should claim and own the genuine power we possess. I chose to take on a title that others had applied as an insult, as a way of reclaiming my value, power, and status. As more of us make this choice to become the most evolved, experienced, and wise form of The Goddess, the meaning that the word Crone holds also evolves.

I want to be part of that evolution!

As I move more deeply into my own Cronehood, I am aware of how much actual power is contained in aging. Women live longer than men and we tend to be healthier, even with the infirmities of aging.

As we age beyond the patriarchal control of men, we are increasingly more personally powerful. Older women are less bound by "propriety" and are more willing to speak their mind and share their opinions. We have more time to run organizations and devote ourselves to our interests. If we work, we have usually chosen to, and even when it is necessary, we have more control over the structure of it and are more willing to risk demanding that control.

With these new eyes, I can now look at Baba Yaga, who so influenced my young life. Of course, She was depicted as fearsome and loathsome! She never relinquished her power. Men who held power elsewhere recognized that and feared her, because they could not control her and needed to rationalize their own fear. Baba Yaga was a shapeshifter and could appear in any guise she wished. I think it suited Her to spend most of Her time as Crone. She also swept away all traces of Her passage as She flew. If She is hard to find, She is hard to hunt down and trap. She could hide in plain sight and survived through the ages. I found her. I have always loved Her, and now choose to become Her.

If we track Church history back far enough into the Old Testament, we find Yahweh or Jehovah still had a wife. Her name was Asherah and She can still be found in *The Book of Kings*. Today in the Middle East, people know her as Astarte and Ishtar, roughly translated as "Sacred Tree." As the scriptures were edited She began to disappear.

To reclaim the Goddess is to reclaim the balance of both The Lord and Lady. The Sacred Marriage or Heiros Gamos has no meaning without both. I serve The Goddess because She has been suppressed for so long.

I chose to reclaim Her.

The Goddess was suppressed through thousands of years of programming, power imposition, violence, and editing. I may not see The Shift fully accomplished in this lifetime, but it is occurring. She is returning, and with each reclaiming She grows. Strong women who wanted more for me than they had, guided me, but accepted the patriarchal boundaries and definitions of who they could be.

As I look at my daughters and granddaughters, I see more for them and a different world. Now it is my turn to advise and steer, and I see them growing beyond The Shift. I always felt the omissions and inconsistencies in the Bible, my faith journey, and Church tradition. The answers never satisfied me, but I never stopped asking and searching for my own answers or seeking ceremony.

As more scholars can unearth the temples and writings of our history, revealing Her in Her glory again, She grows in strength, influence, and power.

The real challenge now is to return to an ancient Eastern tradition of our Deity as all and no gender. The more we reclaim the Divine Feminine and the wisdom and power of The Crone as part of the Divine, the more we will expand. And the more we will embrace the concept of Oneness as I glimpsed it in The Healing Garden in Dachau.

It is something far greater than we can now imagine. In my faith, that is Love.

I come to the Labyrinth seeking The One. I stand in the center. I am SHe. I am Love. I am here now.

ABOUT MICHELE WOODBURN, AUTHOR

As the Queen of Royal Scotsman Auction & Appraisal, I have put my degree in Psychology to good use for the last 26 years, assisting people in the process of divesting themselves of the material accumulations of this life.

Before becoming the Queen, I spent 30 years guiding people labeled as disabled toward finding their wholeness.

I came into this life with the conviction that in spite of differences, we are all whole and all divine. For some of us, that means we need to discover that wholeness to express our divinity. My own journey of discovery is more of an uncovering as I have spent my life seeking my own answers. I walked my first labyrinth as a young woman and found it life-altering. Now that I am in my Cronehood, I am determined to build my own labyrinth.

When I am not at my computer promoting my husband's estate sale business, you will find me out in my garden, working on my labyrinth.

You can find me on FaceBook at The Queen's Court, which will share The Labyrinth at Lavender Cottage as it develops.

REVEALING
BY PAMELA HAWKINS

There I was sitting on the floor holding a deck of goddess cards. I spent some time looking at the beautiful illustrations created by an artist I really admired. I thought about how these cards came to be in my possession as my fingers traced some of the drawings. They had belonged to my mother who had just died unexpectedly a few months earlier, and my heart felt tender to even hold them in my hands.

I had recently decided to be part of a circle of women who were exploring the priestess archetype and deepening our experience of cultivating our inner spiritual authority. We would begin the process with an initiation ceremony. It included writing an Intention statement and aligning with three goddess archetypes to be our guiding and supportive influences for our nine-month journey together.

I had already been working with Persephone, so that was a given. Then I intentionally chose Changing Woman, a Native American figure, as I felt I was going through so many changes in my life. Especially since being rocked to the core when not only my mother but also both grandmothers had all died within a few weeks of each other earlier that year.

So I shuffled this precious deck of cards, asking silently who would be my third goddess. I laid the cards out, picked one, and turned it over to find the name Sedna. I had never heard of her before. After reading the short description of her myth, I thought, "Holy shit, her story is even worse and more frightening than Persephone's!"

The myth of Persephone involves her as a young girl, admiring and picking flowers one day when the earth suddenly opened up and Hades, in his chariot, emerged, captured her, and took her back to the Underworld to be his bride.

Persephone's grief-stricken mother, Demeter, went searching the world over for her daughter. Demeter, or Ceres, was the Goddess of Grain and Agriculture. Once it was discovered that Hades had captured her, she pleaded with Zeus, Persephone's father, to get her back. He refused to intervene. In her grief and rage, Demeter stopped tending to the agriculture on earth and humans began to suffer from a great famine. Zeus eventually interceded, and Hades finally agreed to release Persephone on one condition. If she had not consumed any pomegranate seeds, she could return. She had, however, consumed a few seeds, so a compromise was reached. She was allowed to return to Demeter for six months of the year and be with Hades in the Underworld for the other half of the year. Hence our seasons. When Peresephone returns from the depths, Demeter is happy, and we have spring and summer. Then, fall and winter as the sadness of letting her daughter go again, is represented by the time of nature waning and lying fallow.

Persephone, however, eventually takes her place as the Queen of the Underworld and is one of the few characters in mythology who can move between the worlds.

Now, as I read Sedna's story, it seemed somehow even more horrifying.

Sedna was a beautiful young Inuit woman who lived with her father. He brought many suitors home, but Sedna refused to marry, until one mysterious stranger captivated her attention. He promised to take her away, treat her well, and live in luxury. But upon arriving on his island home, he revealed his true self, a spirit bird creature who had been masquerading as a man. He kept her imprisoned in his nest. Betrayed and miserable, she cried out to her father for help. He came in his canoe and secretly rescued her.

Sedna's escape angered her husband, and he and a flock of birds caused a fierce storm to arise on the sea. Frightened for his life, Sedna's father threw her into the ocean as an offering in hopes of calming the waters. Shocked by her father's actions, Sedna tried to climb back into the boat. Her father chopped off her fingers as she clung to the side, and she fell to the bottom of the frigid sea. As she descended, her fingers became the whales, seals, and all the great creatures of the sea. Now in Adlivum, the Inuit underworld, Sedna rules the dead and is considered the Goddess of the Sea. Hoping she will provide food for the hunters, shamans descend to visit her and show respect by combing her tangled hair and massaging her mutilated hands.

There are many versions of the story across the Arctic regions, but hers is a story of regeneration and she can be seen as a symbol of the nourishing gifts that may be found in the deep, dark, cold places we most fear.

It seemed many messages and experiences in my life were teaching me that I needed to learn and understand what could be gained from going to or being in dark or uncomfortable "places." Death and transformation were destined to be my lifelong Teachers, showing me, ultimately, that while death follows birth in the creation cycle, it doesn't end there. Death is followed by rebirth and life transforms. Something fresh and new may arise out of the deep loss and grief. Just as I was grieving the end of my marriage, I came upon the phrase, "Life is like a circle. What looks like the end is also the beginning."

Sometimes, the stories of our lives take a long arc.

Fast forward twenty years and several astrologers are talking about the importance of the element of water, specifically about two dwarf planets, Salacia and Sedna.

I had known that a small planetary body had been given the name Sedna, but somehow never heard, or connected the dots, that within a few weeks of the time I was sitting on the floor twenty years earlier, divining that Sedna card, a team of astronomers was discovering a dwarf planet. And they were naming it for her, as she travels deeper into space, by far, than any other planetary body we knew of at the time that rotates around the Sun.

She's also the first planet to be named outside of Greco-Roman mythology. Incredibly, it takes 11,400 years for her to complete one trip around the Sun, and her elliptical orbit is highly unusual—close to the Sun at one end of the ellipse and venturing far, far into the deep, frozen outer limits of our galaxy at the other end.

One view of evolutionary astrology is that as we discover new planetary bodies and assign names, meanings, and representations to them, we are "seeing" something for the first time, even though it was there all along.

This implies there's something in our consciousness that is ready to see, grow, and integrate this expanded view of our surroundings into our awareness and ourselves.

It's as if we become bigger to accommodate this new discovery, this new information, this new understanding of reality.

This experience happened for me when my mom died. During a three-day window, as new information came to light about her condition, it became clear she was going to die. So, in this short span of time, I went from asking when we could take her home from the hospital, to talking about moving her to hospice, and then instead, lying with her on the bed as she took her last breath.

I had to adapt rapidly to changing circumstances, let go of my desires, be in shock, and be present for an unbelievable unfolding new reality. I had to move into a space of complete surrender.

I could feel myself expanding to hold new truths every few hours. I could feel myself being impacted at the cellular level and knew I would never be the same.

Suddenly I was thrust into this new reality, reeling. It had only been six weeks since my mother's mother had died, and now she had died. When my other grandmother died a few weeks later, the Matriarchy of my family was gone, leaving me standing there, wobbling like a new foal...as if a cosmic umbilical cord had been cut and I was forced to breathe in a new way.

Surely, this wasn't how it was supposed to go. Right?

What "gifts" could possibly come from this?

It took me a while to have some perspective about this, but ultimately, her death delivered me to a new and unexpected phase of my life. Parts of me were born or came to life because of her passing. The trajectory of my life was impacted. Among many things, I would've never become part of that circle of women and never picked that Sedna card. Lifelong significant relationships sprouted. New areas of interest came to the forefront. I had another layer of awakening as I was going deeper on the journey of becoming more and more my true self. I can trace so many aspects of my life now back to my mother's death. It was Grace that allowed me to know in the moment that her death was simultaneously her spiritual gift to me...and we would continue our connection on different sides of the veil.

With the discovery of the dwarf planet, Sedna, along with several other asteroids and small planets located beyond Pluto in the Kuiper Belt, and further out in the Oort Cloud, we are transforming our understanding of the physical solar system from both an astronomical and an astrological point of view.

The way a person's birth chart is interpreted and how we understand ourselves through this lens is shifting and expanding, as new discoveries are made and names and mythological stories attached to them. While it's understood that we are assigning that meaning, it still gives us a context in which to understand ourselves, to know ourselves, perhaps from a more multi-dimensional and galactic perspective.

And also from the information right in front of us on Earth, as happened one day when I noticed Sedna spelled backward is Andes. The contrast of extremes struck me right away, given that the mountains represent the highest peaks on Earth. I began to consider the range of spatial aspects associated with this archetype. She is way deep "down there" as a goddess at the bottom of the Arctic Ocean; way high "up there" at the mountain peaks; way far "out there" as a planetary body; and the opposite can only lead us way far "in there."

What can we each do to connect with our own inner Sedna, exploring deep inside our bodies? What is hidden, waiting to be revealed?

Before we can go "beyond" the shift, we will shift. Our collective shift will be made up of the shifts each one of us makes and goes through as the Earth evolves. Life, as we have known it, is changing. For some, it's subtle. For others, it may involve huge loss, tragedy, pain, or grief. None of us knows what's ahead. The Unknown generally invokes a feeling of uncertainty, which may invoke a sense of fear or at least not feeling safe or comfortable.

If we take the example of discovering more planetary bodies rotating around our Sun than we were previously aware of, then this new information shatters the understanding we previously had. The maxim says, "As above, so below." If that's the case, then we are in the midst of expanding our awareness of who we are and what we are capable of. And so much more about ourselves is going to come to light through our awareness and knowing.

We're in a dance, a rhythm between knowing and not knowing, between visible and invisible, conscious and unconscious, the finite and the infinite. It's a fluid, moving, shifting dynamic. Can we move gracefully with it?

New discoveries, new information, and new/ancient truths are coming to light. Some of this information is challenging the foundation of our current belief systems and structures. The question doesn't seem to be whether the information is actually true or not, but how will we adapt and incorporate it? Are we willing to expand our beliefs and orientations, our thinking, to match the new revelations? If not, it feels like falling in love with a flower bud and not wanting it to open into its full expression…not allowing it to open up to reveal everything that is held inside.

Just like me in the hospital with my mom all those years ago, we have to expand to hold new understandings. Both about ourselves and us as humans, where we come from, and where we live.

Part of what we can do is practice becoming comfortable in both the known and the unknown.

Even if we're hopeful and excited for what's to come with our expansion in consciousness, it will still involve "change." It will still involve getting out of our comfort zones. The very idea of expanding means that there will be stretching and sometimes breaking. Something will die, and something new will be born from that ending.

Can we become the magical cosmic child and approach this with curiosity rather than constriction?

There's so much we can learn about ourselves by witnessing nature, the cycles that occur on the Earth and in the sky.

Every 18 months, the planet Venus shifts from being an evening star to a morning star. She shines brightly in the night sky and then disappears from view for a time before re-emerging, becoming visible in the morning sky just before sunrise. The time in between, when she's not seen— this apparent descent—corresponds to the ancient Sumerian myth of Inanna (Venus), known as the Queen of Heaven.

The story, as told in a poem, begins with the Queen Inanna, in Heaven, turning her ear toward the Great Below. Seeking perhaps to extend her power to this Underworld realm ruled by her sister, she heeds the call of the Great Below and begins her descent.

The sister, Ereshkigal, is not pleased with the news and orders the seven gates of the Underworld bolted. The only way Inanna can proceed is to remove a piece of her royal garment before she can pass through each gate, one by one. By the time Inanna reaches the Underworld, she is naked and powerless. Overpowered by her sister, she's turned into a corpse and put on a hook.

She is eventually revived, and after some negotiation about another taking her place, she emerges anew. As does Venus in the sky, re-emerging as a morning star from her descent into darkness.

The story, which predates the Greek myth of Persephone and Demeter, also involves a relationship to the cycle of the seasons.

Like all myths and ancient stories, there are many versions, interpretations, and meanings to ponder. The significant parts that resonate with me include this feeling of the call of the Below, the Depth, the Unknown—of us, our emotions, our vulnerability, our nakedness. Sometimes the sister, Ereshkigal, is seen as a disowned aspect of Inanna, seeking to be reconnected and re-integrated.

When we find ourselves in a "dark night of the soul" or a descent into our own Underworld, there may be a part of us seeking to reconnect with lost parts of ourselves. We may be forced to surrender something of ourselves in order to re-emerge with a new sense of ourselves, mining a gift from our deep dive.

We may often want to avoid going "down there." Still we must remember that literally, all precious metals and jewels are underground. And figuratively, we must be willing to go down there to retrieve and receive our own precious inner gifts, our divine gold and diamonds.

Once in my own "dark night," I was at such a low time in my life. There was no crisis, but I just couldn't feel any kind of enthusiasm about my life or purpose for being. I couldn't find any magic inside. I felt so horrible about myself... so inadequate, humiliated, depressed...such a failure. So

UNable. Immersed in my own inner hell. I don't know what else to call it but Despair.

One morning, waking yet again in my unbearable shittiness of being, I tried, of all things, writing a gratitude list. A friend had suggested it the night before. My eye-rolling, adolescent self was in no mood, thinking the whole thing was stupid. But I tried anyway. I tried to come up with ten things that I could muster some kind of appreciation for. In doing it, though, I actually felt something shift. Something began to lighten, just a tiny bit.

Somehow that tiny shift created a crack, maybe that oft-mentioned crack where the light gets in. Or maybe just enough of a crack for me to pass through to another dimension of this dark place. And so began a day-long conversation with my deep self and what I can only describe as my Wise Council.

These wise beings were meeting me in this darkest place, at my emotional rock-bottom, having a raw "get real" moment with myself. The Wise Council simply asked me, "What do you want?" It seemed so simple, yet so profound. Their presence with me was so complete and non-judgmental.

I had this feeling like when you just scrape away all the bullshit and get down to the true heart of the matter, "What do you really want?"

I felt like I was wiping everything off the table, so to speak. Getting to a blank slate, starting with nothing, and then adding what I wanted one by one. Just the basic, true, fundamental things that I want. Mostly this all had to do with my life's purpose and sacred work. In this communion, this presence, I was digging around in the deep recesses and muck. I was searching for, identifying, my deepest desires about how I wanted to live. How I wanted to be in this world, what I wanted to honor and celebrate about the nature of life and each of us...our uniqueness.

Basically, it boiled down to three things: I wanted to express my divine gifts, receive compensation from them to provide for myself and my children, and from that exchange to give something forward, to contribute toward making the world a better place.

How could I do this? I thought about painting flowers, but the truth is, I could paint a flower one time and be "done with that," so I honed even further. For whatever reason, there is one flower, the Calla Lily, which captivated me, and I knew I could draw or paint it again and again. It was like a vein of gold for me.

But I didn't want to just paint flowers. I wanted it to mean something *more*. I wrote down tenets that were related to growth and blossoming, like Nature does, that felt important to me. Thinking about the Earth as Eden, as a garden planet, and that each one of us is a unique and incredible blossom in that garden.

I wrote a short manifesto with all that I wanted to be infused in this project. I made a commitment to myself to paint nothing but lilies for one year. I felt so energetically beleaguered at the time, so it had to be something that also felt manageable and that I would follow through with.

BEYOND THE SHIFT

Little by little, moment by moment, small pieces of me came to life, and I felt inspired, truly In-spirit-ed. By the end of the day, I had a name for this project, The Lily Movement, and set my intention of creating a global garden. I felt "on purpose" like I hadn't in a long time.

And I did fulfill that commitment. For even longer than a year, I painted lilies and sold them. I donated money to organizations doing good work in the world, such as planting trees in the Amazon Rainforest, teaching children about food gardens at school, and to humanitarian organizations. I created a body of work that brought Beauty to the world. There was beauty in the images, and in the soulfully inspired undertone of the project infused into each piece.

But the part I feel is most important for me to remember is that this beauty of mine was found and born within my deepest pain, from my deepest existential wound of inadequacy. I literally became the adage of the beautiful lotus flower that emerges from the dank, dark, muddy soil.

And there is now the embodied knowing that there is a gift in the pain, there is a vein of gold in the darkness of the unknown, there is always a seed of potential lying deep in our underground. And we may find it whether we feel called to descend or whether life thrusts us into a cruel circumstance.

Like a seed giving way to a visible sprout that was previously unseen, I imagine part of the reason Sedna was discovered twenty years ago is that she is ready to be seen (again). She is approaching the Sun on her return from the outer reaches of deep space. She will be closer to Earth over the next fifty years than she has been in thousands of years. She has traveled through territory that is beyond our imagination. And I believe we are readying ourselves to see her and receive the messages from her journey into deep space.

I can't help but think she is like a traveler who's been on an extremely long expedition and returning to us with the news of her voyage. Ancient civilizations may have been aware of her as a planetary body, but if so, she has been lost to history until now.

Perhaps it's time for Sedna to emerge from the bottom of the ocean and take her place in the celestial realms. Honored as a sister who has traveled so far away and returns to us with a message from the furthest reaches of Earth's solar system. What is she bringing us?

Imagine someone approaching you from far, far away. They appear as a tiny speck. As they approach, they appear larger as they come closer. You begin to see various features. They may look strange to you. They've been somewhere further away than you can imagine. As she gets closer, it seems she has something for you, perhaps in her outstretched hands, or she may want to tell you something. What is it? How do you feel about this stranger? Do you want to run away? Are you open and curious?

Now, imagine this entity, this being, is emerging from somewhere deep inside of you. It is you. It's the eternal you bearing a message, a new vision, a new awareness and remembrance. To re–member is to gather all the parts of you buried in the depths of your bones, your psyche, your cosmic history and weave them back together. And you're ready to expand into a greater awareness. You actually become the luminosity to reveal this—your inner divine secrets.

You are dying from what you've known thus far, and you are transforming to contain a new reality—a new awareness of the grand multi-dimensional Creator Being you are.

While there's betrayal in Persephone's kidnapping, assumed rape, and initial turning away of her father, there's a bittersweet awe that she eventually claims her sovereignty as Queen of the Underworld and becomes a multi-dimensional traveler and shapeshifter.

It's excruciating to think of Sedna's fingers being chopped off by her own father. And yet achingly beautiful that those fingers turn into beloved sea creatures who also sacrifice themselves for the sustenance of the people.

It's poignant to think about the despair of a dark night giving birth to Inspiration and Beauty. Knowing this helps when I experience uncomfortable feelings and sensations.

Sometimes when I wake up, the first thing I feel is a nervous tension in my body—around the solar plexus area and also the vagus nerve bundle. One recent morning, I had the impression to become small and transport myself to sit right in the midst of that area of my body and just notice, with my inner holy gaze.

It made me think of Sedna's tangled hair and how the shamans descend to the bottom of the frozen sea to comb it out, as a way of showing reverence.

REVEALING

So I went down to comb the tangles inside myself.

I'm sitting in the middle of what feels like a
tangled nerve bundle.
Just witnessing and noticing.

Feeling . . .   Breathing . . .

Asking for more space with each breath.
Opening up the constriction a little more
with each breath.

I saw myself combing through the
ratted nerve bundle, bit by bit,
bringing tenderness and compassion to the
places inside that feel scared, anxious, insecure.

There's a little regret here, a little remorse there,
some humiliation, some worry, and uncertainty.

And with each untangling and
separation of the strands,
they begin to turn to gold threads.

I take a breath as I acknowledge that sometimes
it feels more safe to stay in the cave than to
come out into the sun . . .   Light.

And I breathe in peace and exhale stress.
And I breathe in peace and exhale peace . . .
right into all those ratted tangles.

BEYOND THE SHIFT

Combing . . .   Combing . . .
Letting memories come up.
Combing . . .   Singing . . .
Singing a soul song.

Breathing in peace, exhaling a whisper . . .
softly blowing into grievances old, even ancient.

Breathing . . .   Singing . . .   Calling . . .
Calling the Me of me.

Combing . . .   Calling . . .

Calling in the memory . . .
Calling the eternal Me of me home.

Combing, breathing, calling, singing . . .
Singing a soul song to remember who I was
before I forgot . . .
To remember who I am.

Combing and Calling . . .

And as the knots untangle,
I comb the golden threads and . . .
they become fibers of Light.

Combing . . .   and Weaving . . .   and Drawing . . .

Drawing and weaving the fibers of Light
into a new constellation

REVEALING

in the soul sky that lives
deep deep deep in my belly . . .
deep deep deep in my heart . . .
deep deep deep in my bones.

Reclaiming the creative power that was
tamped down, forgotten, subverted, repressed.

Re-organizing . . .   Restructuring . . .
Restoring . . .
Remembering . . .

Remembering.
Remembering.
Remembering.

I feel we must be willing to sit in the middle of our tangled vagus nerve bundle, or our deepest feelings of betrayal... resentment...grief. And feel and listen and breathe and love.

As with Sedna, we can explore deep into outer space, and we can dive deep into our own inner space. The further we go into space, the deeper we can go inside ourselves, and vice versa.

We have to be willing to ask where we have taken too much responsibility or not enough. We have to be willing to go "down there" into the "basement" of the situation and bring our flashlight. We have to be willing to release ourselves from old contracts that place too much restriction, and be willing to write new ones of liberation and sovereignty. And to acknowledge when it is you and only you who can do that for yourself.

Frozen emotions need to thaw, emerge, and be expressed.

The unlovable parts of ourselves need to be Loved.

The limitations we've placed on ourselves, intentionally or unintentionally, need to be lifted.

The veils will drop or dissolve and a revealing will take place.

What fascinates me is that so much more exists, and has forever, but is still unknown to us...yet unrevealed.

Right now, when I imagine going into the depths, the darkest places in my body, the hidden places inside my bones and cells, it feels like gold to be discovered there and even golden doorways to infinite new worlds and possibilities.

New discoveries feel like waking up and remembering that feeling of knowing something, but you don't know what it is. We are all on a journey of self-discovery, planetary discovery, cosmic discovery, and remembering our true nature... that of a Creator Being.

As we continue to explore and be curious and nurture our pioneering spirits, more and more will naturally be revealed, and more and more, we will be able to expand to hold new truths, new realities, new capabilities...new dimensional thought and travel. New and ancient gifts will be activated inside of us.

May we hear the call. When the great below is calling, may

we descend into the darkness of nothingness and surrender all preconceived ideas of who we are. So we can melt into the jelly mass of no form, and emerge with the Knowledge of all that we are and ever have been. May we be willing to go beyond our imagination.

We are on an inner expedition, harnessing our pioneering spirits and our creative warrior hearts. Riding the Earth Dragon into her new era of lighted crystalline awareness and Co-Creation. From that place, we no longer seek to live a divine plan but rather live AS creation, as divine artists and architects, poets and musicians, as divine Humans writing our future on the magnificent blank canvas of infinity lying before us.

What will we create?

ABOUT PAMELA HAWKINS, AUTHOR

First, I want to acknowledge and give thanks to all the people in my life who have written, said, or phrased things in such a way that touched me and awakened little threads of magic inside. Truthfully, I hope that my own writing and art does the same for others.

My creativity has long been a part of my life. As a graphic designer, I have helped clients bring their visions, books, products, and messages into form.

As an art medicine woman, I've helped people explore and discover their own natural creativity and experience deep healing, transformation, and profound joy in personal and spiritual growth through authentic expression.

As a design teacher, I've woven all of my experience together to help my students become good visual communicators and enhance their aesthetic sensibilities.

Currently, I'm focusing on what wants to come through me—my Signature Work, as a conduit between Source and the material world. At heart, I'm a messenger and visual translator of soul language—the ethereal. It's poignant that so much of my life has been around visual arts and communication, as I have also struggled along the way with my own visibility, being seen. Even so, I am devoted to bringing forth that which will deeply touch, inspire, and activate our inherent true nature—the luminous Creator Being that is each of us.

Website: www.pamelahawkins.com

AFTERWORD

You are on a journey that is uniquely your own, yet an intrinsic piece of the puzzle that completes the whole. The oneness that inherently exists because you exist.

In 2014, three years after I lost my corporate publishing job with Wiley Canada, I was doing a jigsaw puzzle. It occurred to me as we lay out all the pieces that we register it all at a higher level. As we build it, we examine each piece individually, trying to make it fit—we test it by shape and colour markings. And suddenly, we insert ten, fifteen, twenty pieces in rapid succession. I shared my discovery with my partner, who thought I'd lost my mind when I said, "Oh my goodness, our subconscious mind maps out the entire puzzle, and our conscious mind tries to make the pieces fit."

Isn't this a magnificent mirror for life?

I knew I had a mission, but it eluded me as I looked externally to where I "fit."

The "pieces" come in nudges, suggestions, dreams, and synchronicities. After losing my job, I kept getting tapped on the shoulder to work with people to find their voices, their value, and to share their stories and publish their sacred books. It was a daunting task, and just because I'd spent 31 years in the industry didn't mean I could take new authors from concept to celebration.

Until I realized books had been my entire life's focus. I belonged here as a Spiritual Librarian, word whisperer, and book publisher. Within a month after deciding this was

AFTERWORD

indeed my work to do, my first client—Marie Martin—signed on and I published four spiritual books in my first year.

It's how alignment works. Our higher self and our human self see the "pieces." And we take action.

I saw this in real time on March 24, 2023, when a fun little TikTok jump-started the collaboration that was about to unfold. The result is this book you hold in your hand.

The idea and name, Beyond The Shift, came to me two years prior. I knew the year before I started my publishing company that, one day, I'd create an anthology. It would be a series that each author would be so freaking proud of and honoured to be a part of. We would all grow personally and professionally, and we would have a mutual intention to help shift the collective consciousness.

I am so proud of this accomplishment, and the series birthed so long ago as a dream and then a knowing. I knew twelve talented Spiritual Entrepreneurs would say yes. And they did, and we got to work. Thank you to the incredible authors who penned their name to Beyond The Shift, Volume One.

And thank you, dear reader and friends, who believed in us and the concept that has shifted as all great ideas do: from an idea in the quantum field into physical form. May you live in the possibilities and probabilities of life and know at a cellular level—every single moment—that you belong.

With love and gratitude,
Pamela Lynch

ABOUT THE AUTHORS

WENDY S. BURTON

Being a published author is a dream fulfilled, and Wendy hopes to make this her new career calling. She is now a two-time author in 2023, with the publication of her first novel, Amy and the Angels.

She only knew how to achieve this personal goal through what she had always done—enlist the help of her Angels.

Website: https://www.wendysburton.com

KARINA GARCIA DEL PEZO, ACM

Karina Garcia Del Pezo, ACM, is the Founder of Terra Nova Crystals, an online crystal shop. She helps people connect to their soul crystals through live sales and private consultations.

Karina teaches online spiritual courses and workshops, and also provides Shamanic Crystal Reiki healing sessions.

Website: https://terranovacrystals.rocks

INGRID TOLEDO-HAMMETT

Ingrid Toledo-Hammett is passionate about assisting those who suffer from indoctrination, complex trauma, or other forms of attachment. As a Reiki Master Teacher, she offers live and pre-recorded courses in English and Spanish.

She is Agua Viva; Ingrid Witch One and brings her brand of magick and spiritual tools using mediumship, remote viewing, and meditation.

Website: https://www.botanica-aguaviva.com

LUCIE MIŁOSZ HASKINS

Lucie Haskins is a lifelong student of how to live an expanded life full of freedom, integrity, and learning. She enjoys awakening others to what's possible in their lives and to the innate power we each have within us.

She's lived an eclectic life and career—first as a young Polish immigrant learning how to fit into a new culture in America to later experiencing life as a military wife, computer programmer, management consultant, freelance indexer and editor, and finally writer.

Pamela Hawkins

Pamela Hawkins is an artist, an author, an explorer of mystery, a dreamer, and a visionary. She is devoted to discovering deep soul truths and expressing them in a way that touches and inspires others as we move through our individual and planetary evolution.

Website: https://www.pamelahawkins.com

Sarah Holmes

Sarah has a gift for holding space and impacting clients by listening deeply to their words, language, and heart, as she guides them to their inner lantern. Sarah uses a modality called Biodynamic Cranial Sacral, which helps with trauma held in the body.

She is a Certified Meditation teacher and Sound Healing Guide and has created her own tool box of modalities for clients.

Email: essentialwellnesswithin@gmail.com

Katrina Laflin

Katrina Laflin is on a mission to help you find your true identity, align with your highest potential, and live a life that resonates with your authentic self.

Katrina's favorite tool to guide you on your journey of discovery is Numerology. It brought her to embrace her own Radical Authenticity. Katrina calls it her SoulScape.

Website: https://livingyoursoulscape.com
Email: createyoursoulscape@gmail.com

Libby Lee

Libby Lee is a visionary on a mission to empower people to align with their authenticity, find clarity in their mission, and radiate their light into the world.

Her profound insights into the spiritual and personal development world have led her to understand the crucial role that authenticity plays in one's journey to self-discovery and empowerment.

Website: https://www.libbylee.com.au

Heather Middler

Heather's ability to tune into the connection between Souls is an incredible gift, and as an End of Life Doula, it gives her immense satisfaction to be with her clients during this sensitive and emotional time of transition.

Heather often continues to work with her clients after their loved one transitions.

Email: hmiddler868@yahoo.com

Angela Kaye Simon, B.A., B.S., M.A., G.C., PhD(c-abd)

Angela has had a long and successful interdisciplinary career. She began her career in academia as a sociologist, professor, and researcher.

After suffering an accident in 2009, Angela transitioned herself full-time into entrepreneurship. She now runs multiple businesses as an international spiritual leader, coach, and influencer. When she's not working and running her businesses, she can be found gardening, volunteering, playing with her cat, and building her eco-homestead.

Website: https://www.TheIntuitiveCreatrix.com

Tara Winter

Tara Winter is an intuitive energy reader, astrologer, and healer who has a natural gift for connecting with the unseen world. She brings through messages from your guides, past loved ones, and pets, providing you with comfort, closure, and validation.

Tara is available for psychic readings or to learn about your birth chart. To learn more, you can head to Tara's web page:

https://simplytara.my.canva.site

Michele Woodburn

Michele is a semi-retired entrepreneur with 30 years experience helping people solve their problems by guiding them towards their own solutions. Her Psychology degree with a focus in Human Development supports her conviction that each of us is created whole, we just need to discover it.

You can find Michele on FaceBook at The Queen's Court, and she will share The Labyrinth at Lavender Cottage as it develops.

About the Publisher

Pamela Lynch spent 31 years in traditional book publishing, and founded SourceCode Publishing in 2018. She inspires Spiritual Entrepreneurs to become gifted writers and published authors so they can connect with their ideal clients and create a fulfilling life and thriving business.

You can reach Pamela at https://www.pamelalynch.com

www.ingramcontent.com/pod-product-compliance
Lightning Source LLC
Chambersburg PA
CBHW070019100426
42740CB00013B/2555